Focused support for every student

D0998058

WJEC GCSE
English and English Language

Foundation

Stuart Sage

Ted Snell

Nick Duncan

Spoken language consultant:

Jane Hingley

www.pearsonschools.co.uk

✓ Free online support
✓ Useful weblinks
✓ 24 hour online ordering

0845 630 22 22

Heinemann

Part of Pearson

Heinemann is an imprint of Pearson Education Limited, a company incorporated in England and Wales, having its registered office at Edinburgh Gate, Harlow, Essex, CM20 2JE. Registered company number: 872828

www.pearsonschoolsandfecolleges.co.uk

Heinemann is a registered trademark of Pearson Education Limited

First published 2010

14 13 12
10 9 8 7 6 5

British Library Cataloguing in Publication Data
A catalogue record for this book is available from the British Library

ISBN 978 0 435016 86 9

Websites
The websites used in this book were correct and up-to-date at the time of publication. It is essential for tutors to preview each website before using it in class so as to ensure that the URL is still accurate, relevant and appropriate.

Edited by Jeremy Toynbee
Designed and produced by Kamae Design, Oxford
Cover design by Wooden Ark Studios, Leeds
Original illustrations © Pearson Education Limited 2010
Illustrated by Kamae Design and Rory Walker
Picture research by Zooid Pictures
Cover photo © SA TEAM/FN/Minden/FLPA
Printed and bound by Ashford Colour Press Ltd, Gosport, Hants

Acknowledgements
We would like to thank the schools that were involved in this project for their invaluable help creating exam answers for this book.

The authors and publisher would like to thank the following individuals and organisations for permission to reproduce material in this book:

p9 Zooid Pictures; p11 Steven von Niederhausern/iStockphoto; p15 Tony French/Alamy; p16 Mark Whitfield/Rex Features; p18 Justin Kase zsixz/Alamy; p22 Bernie Pearson/Alamy; p24 LOOK Die Bildagentur der Fotografen GmbH/ Alamy; p26 Shenval/Alamy; p30 Photofusion Picture Library/Alamy; p33 Peter Coombs/Alamy; p35 David R. Frazier Photolibrary, Inc./Alamy; p38 Mercury Press Agency Ltd; p40 Mark Bolton/Corbis UK Ltd; p43 Photolibrary Group; p46 Denis Jones/Evening Standard/Rex Features; p57 Everyday Images/ Alamy; p59 Visual Image Photographic Services/JORVIK Viking Centre, York Archaeological Trust; p63 Monaco Palace/Getty Images; p67 Henry Iddon/ Alamy; p68 Photolibrary Group; p71 Rex Features; p72 Digital Vision; p73 Caroline Penn/WaterAid; p73 Frantzesco Kangaris/Epa. Corbis UK Ltd; p73 Peter Radacsi, Shutterstock; p77 Andrew Harrington/Alamy; p80 East News/ Rex Features; p83 Elmtree Images/Alamy; p85 Bernie Pearson/Alamy; p87 Wild Life Ranger/Alamy; p90 T.M.O.Travel/Alamy; p92 Phanie Agency/ Rex Features; p97 Marnie Burkhart/Corbis UK Ltd; p98 Zooid Pictures; p100 Ian Shaw/Alamy; p101 PCL/Alamy; p105 Images & Stories/Alamy; p109 Blend Images/Alamy; p112 Zooid Pictures; p115 lemonlight features/Alamy;

p118 Janine Wiedel Photolibrary/Alamy; p121 Paula Solloway/Alamy; p126 Wildscape/Alamy; p132 UpperCut Images/Alamy; p135 Ted Foxx. Alamy; p139 Roger Bamber/Alamy; p140 Universal Pictures/Ronald Grant Archive; p143 Bettmann/Corbis UK Ltd.; p148 Ned Coomes/Zooid Pictures; p154 keith morris. Alamy ; p159 Tony Wear/Shutterstock; p159 Elnur/Shutterstock; p160 Associated Press/Press Association Images; p164 Zooid Pictures; p169 Geoff du Feu/Alamy.

'Britain has gone bananas', reproduced by permission of The Guardian News & Media Ltd. 'How Jamie saved me', by Amelia Hill, from the *Guardian* © 22 December 2002, reproduced by permission of The Guardian News & Media Ltd. From a leaflet by the Royal National Lifeboat Institution, reproduced by permission of the RNLI. Bradford Brochure, reproduced by permission of The Department of Culture, Tourism and Sport, City of Bradford Metropolitan District Council. 'Family fun at Centre Parcs', by Robert Lindsay, reproduced by permission of the *Daily Express*. 'Thugs consider ASBOs a "Diploma", report says', by James Slack, from the *Daily Mail* © 2 December 2006, reproduced by permission of the *Daily Mail*. 'Warwick Castle visit', by Lisa Smith, from the *Birmingham Mail* © 2 March 2002, reproduced by permission of the *Birmingham Mail*. 'Half of children never go out', by Laura Clark, from the *Daily Mail* © 13 August 2009, reproduced by permission of the *Daily Mail*. From *Notes from a Small Island*, by Bill Bryson, published by Black Swan, reprinted by permission of The Random House Group Ltd. 'Chris Moyles interview: radio's best kept secret?', by Nigel Farndale, from the *Daily Telegraph* © 14 July 2009, reproduced by permission of The Telegraph Media Limited © 2007/2009. 'A GCSE in frustration', by Tony Barrett, from the *Daily Telegraph* © 26 May 2009, reproduced by permission of The Telegraph Media Limited © 2007/2009. 'Remote control', by Andrew Purvis, from *Observer Life* © 8 March 1998, reproduced by permission of The Guardian News & Media Ltd. Review: 'Family fun at Center Parcs', by Robert Lindsay, source: www.ciao.co.uk, reproduced by permission of Ciao UK. Leaflet: Jorvik Viking Centre, reproduced by permission of Jorvik Viking Centre. 'The show must go on', by Dea Birkett, from the *Guardian* © 6 February 1999, reproduced by permission of The Guardian News & Media Ltd. From a leaflet 'Blackpool: feel the buzz', courtesy of Visit Blackpool. From a web page 'Welcome to Greater Yarmouth', reproduced by permission of Great Yarmouth Borough Council, Tourism Division. From a web page 'Welcome to Southend-on-Sea', reproduced with permission of Southend-on-Sea Borough Council. From a web page 'Ilfracombe North Devon's Premier Resort', reproduced by permission of Ilfracombe & District Tourism Association. Headline: 'Going the distance', by Anne Johnson, from the *Guardian* 6 April 2004, used by permission of Anne Johnson. Headline: 'Let's get fizzical', by Nick Dorman, from the *Daily Mirror* 6 December 2009, reproduced by permission of Mirrorpix. Headline: 'Just 16 actors per episode as EastSpenders is forced to cut back', from the *Daily Mail* 18 October 2009, reproduced by permission of the *Daily Mail*. Headline: 'Even monkeys can get A levels', from the *Metro* 16 August 2009, reproduced by permission of the *Metro*. 'Give water. Give life. Give £2 a month', source: www.wateraid.org.uk, reproduced by permission of WaterAid. Logo: the Oxfam GB logo on page 75 is reproduced with the permission of Oxfam GB, Oxfam House, John Smith Drive, Cowley, Oxford OX4 2JY, UK www. oxfam.org.uk. Oxfam GB does not necessarily endorse any text or activities that accompany the materials. Logo: 'Believe in Barnardo's', reproduced by permission of Barnardo's. Barnardo's Reg. Charity Nos. 216250 and SC037605. Logo: RSPB, reproduced by permission of the RSPB. Logo: WaterAid, source: www.wateraid.org.uk, reproduced by permission of WaterAid. From a leaflet Warwick Castle, reproduced by permission of the Management of Warwick Castle. 'Whaling in the Faroe Islands', article from the High North Alliance Bradford Brochure, reproduced by permission of The Department of Culture, Tourism and Sport, City of Bradford Metropolitan District Council. From *Notes from a Small Island*, by Bill Bryson, published by Black Swan, reprinted by permission of The Random House Group Ltd. 'Safety for parents and child carers', from www.directgov.uk/firekills. 'Inter group GCSE English – speaking and listening training and guidance', reproduced by permission of WJEC. Leaflet: Sandringham, reproduced with permission of Sandringham Estates.

Every effort has been made to contact copyright holders of material reproduced in this book. Any omissions will be rectified in subsequent printings if notice is given to the publishers.

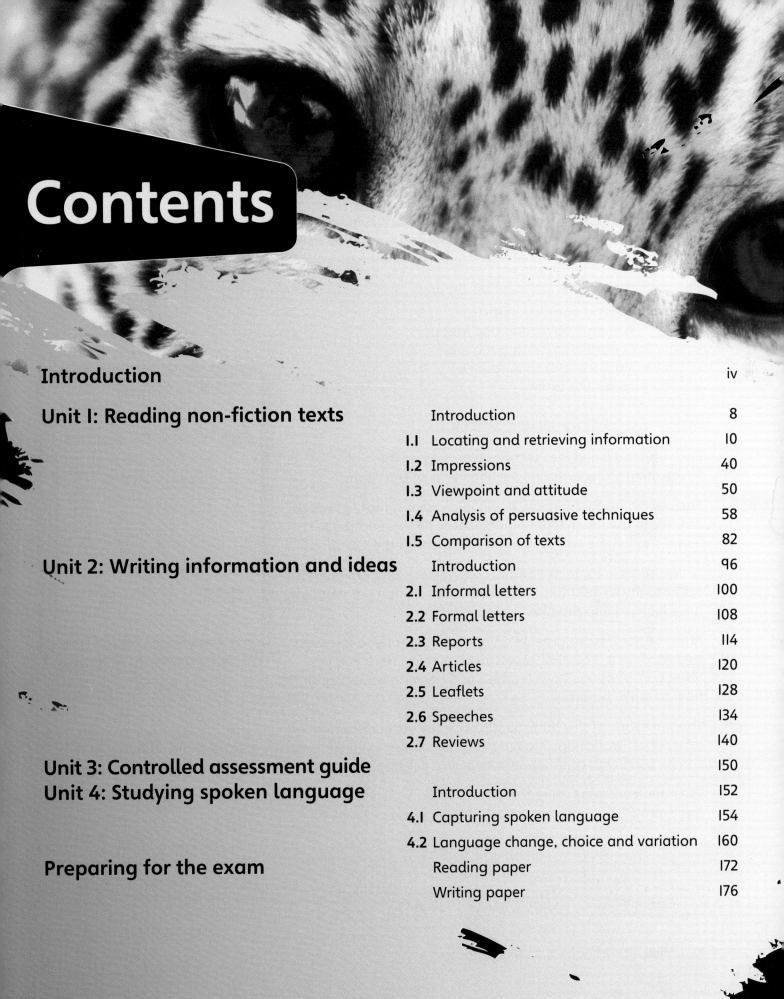

Contents

Introduction

This book is designed to help you raise your achievement in the WJEC GCSE English and GCSE English Language foundation tier exams and controlled assessment tasks. It is tailored to the requirements of the specifications to help you improve your learning.

The book is divided into the following units:

- Unit I: Reading non-fiction texts
- Unit 2: Writing information and ideas
- Unit 3: Controlled assessment guide
- Unit 4: Studying spoken language
- Preparing for the exam.

How does this book work?

Each unit is divided into sections which cover the Assessment Objectives and requirements of the exams.

Each section is then broken down into lessons, most of which open with their own learning objectives ('Your learning'). The lessons teach the skills you need to do well in the exam.

GradeStudio is contained within most lessons and provides an opportunity to read sample student answers and put what you have learned into practice.

Many of the lessons provide an opportunity for you to assess your work in a 'Peer/Self-assessment' activity. Here you can reflect on what you have learned and begin to understand how to make progress.

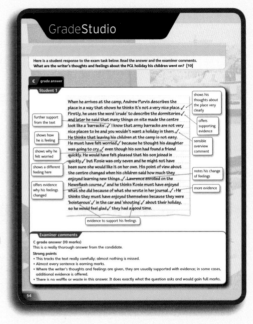

The approach of this book builds on many years of examining experience, workshops, training sessions and revision courses with teachers and students. It can be used with confidence to help you develop and achieve your potential.

We hope you enjoy using this book and find it useful in developing your skills. Good luck in the exams.

Ted Snell, Stuart Sage and Nick Duncan

What is in the exams?

You will have to take two exams in order to complete either GCSE English or GCSE English Language. These are as follows.

	Unit I: Reading non-fiction texts	Unit 2: Writing information and ideas
How long is the exam?	I hour	I hour
What is in the exam?	There are two passages to read – a media text and a non-fiction text. There will be four questions on the texts, each carrying ten marks but occasionally there will be two questions worth five marks and three worth ten marks each. The final question will always ask you to compare the texts in some way.	There are two tasks to complete both of which will be transactional/discursive in nature, e.g. letters, reports, articles, leaflets, reviews. Each task will be marked out of 20 so you should divide your time equally. Across the two tasks you will be asked to write for a range of audiences and purposes.
How much should I write?	It depends on the size of your handwriting, but aim to write about half to one side for each answer.	It depends on the size of your handwriting, but aim to write one to two sides for each answer.
How will I be assessed?	All exams have what are known as 'assessment criteria', which define what is being tested by the questions.	
What are the assessment criteria?	Assessment Objective 2 • Read and understand texts, selecting material appropriate to purpose, collating from different sources and making comparisons and cross-references as appropriate. • Develop and sustain interpretations of writers' ideas and perspectives. • Explain and evaluate how writers use linguistic, grammatical, structural and presentational features to achieve effects and engage and influence the reader.	Assessment Objective 3 • Write clearly and effectively, using and adapting forms and selecting vocabulary appropriate to task and purpose in ways which engage the reader. • Organise information and ideas into structured and sequenced sentences and paragraphs using a variety of features. to give clarity and cohesion to your work. • Use a range of sentence structures for clarity, purpose and effect, with accurate punctuation and spelling. NB One third of the marks for each writing activity is allocated to this last bullet point.

What is in controlled assessment?

For GCSE English, in your written controlled assessment you will be asked to complete the following activities:

- an essay linking a Shakespeare play and poetry. For this piece, you may write about any Shakespeare play and a range of poetry from the WJEC Poetry Collection
- an essay on a Different Cultures prose text taken from the GCSE English Literature set text list. Your teacher will tell you which text you are studying
- a piece of first-person writing
- a piece of third-person writing.

For GCSE English Language, in your controlled assessment you will be asked to write:

- an essay on a novel or play taken from the GCSE English Literature set text list or any play by Shakespeare (except the two listed in the GCSE English Literature set text list). Your teacher will tell you which text you are studying
- a piece of descriptive writing
- a piece of narrative/expressive writing.

For both GCSE English and GCSE English Language, you will have to complete three Speaking and Listening assignments:

- communicating and adapting language (probably an individual presentation)
- interacting and communicating (probably group work)
- creating and sustaining roles (role-play).

If you are taking GCSE English Language, you will also have to complete a Spoken language study.

You will find more information on pages 150–151. Unit 4 (pages 152–171) will help you with the skills needed for the Speaking and Listening assignments.

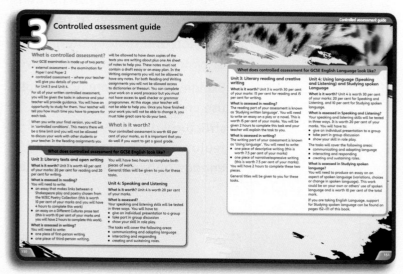

What additional resources are there?

- **Teacher Guide** with full-colour lesson plans and schemes of work, written by an experienced teacher, Sarah Donnelly. These lesson plans make use of the BBC video clips and other resources in the ActiveTeach CD-ROM as well as providing support for EAL students. There is also additional controlled assessment guidance for teachers written by Stuart Sage and Nick Duncan.

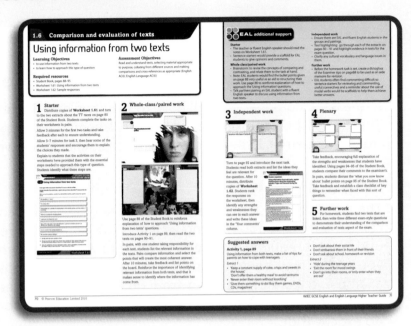

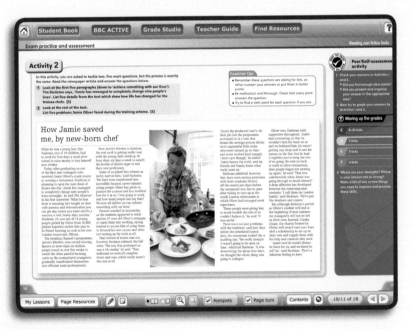

- **ActiveTeach CD-ROM** an on-screen version of the student book together with BBC video clips and other resources including interactive activities, handouts and the full Teacher Guide.

1 Reading non-fiction texts

What will the Reading paper look like?

In the Reading paper you will have to read two non-literary texts on a particular theme. These could be, for example, adverts, factsheets, newspaper or magazine articles, pages from the Internet, leaflets or essays (for example, travel writing).

What will the questions be like?

The questions fall into different, but quite predictable, categories. One way that you can be confident about doing well in these exams is to recognise the type of question and what it requires. You need to prepare yourself by practising the types of questions you are likely to be asked using a range of different kinds of reading material. For example, a leaflet is different from an essay, and you need to be confident about how to approach various kinds of texts. This section of the book is designed to help you to do exactly that.

Only **five** basic types of question are asked in this exam. Examples of these appear opposite. If you practise answering them, then you should be well prepared and able to face the exam with confidence.

How will I be assessed?

The examiner will assess your answers against the assessment criteria outlined on page v.

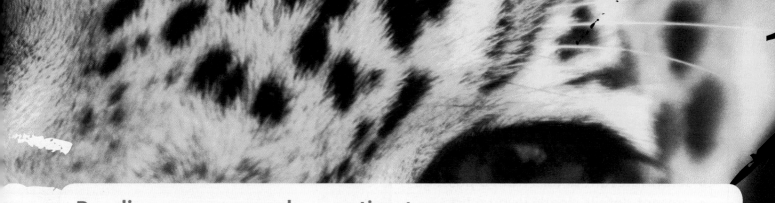

Reading paper sample question types

Below are some examples of the types of question you could be asked in the Reading paper. These will help you understand what you are preparing for as you work through this section of the book.

1 Locating and retrieving information

- List reasons or details/Make a list of...
- Find specific details in the text...
- What evidence does the writer use...?
- Explain what or why or how...

2 Impressions

- What impressions do you get of the writer?
- What impressions do you get of an organisation or people?
- What impressions do you get of a place?

3 Viewpoint and attitude

- What are the writer's attitudes to...?
- What are the writer's opinions of...?
- What are the writer's thoughts and feelings about...?

4 Analysis of persuasive techniques

- How does the writer try to encourage/ interest/argue...?
- How does this text try to persuade/sell/ influence/show...?

5 Comparison of texts

- Compare and contrast these texts.
- Using information from both texts, explain why...

Locating and retrieving information

Your learning

This lesson will help you to:

- select relevant details from a passage
- present details clearly using a list.

List or find questions

List or find questions are usually the first question on the exam paper. This type of question is a good opportunity to gain marks quickly. You need to read the passage carefully and closely.

- You will often be asked to **list** or **find** relevant details from the passage.
- You will gain a mark for each correct point identified.
- You do not have to write in continuous prose. Simply number or bullet point each separate detail or point you make.

Activity 1

Read the extracts opposite, taken from two newspapers, and answer the 'List and find' question from the exam paper below.

List ten separate things mentioned in the two extracts that help explain why bananas are so popular. [10]

(Note that questions worth ten marks will need to be completed in about 12–13 minutes.)

Follow the three steps shown in the table below. Do this whenever you are asked to list or find details from the text.

	What you have to do	Try it out!
1	<ul><li>Check the wording of the question carefully.</li><li>Know what you have to find.</li><li>You may be asked to look at just part of the text.</li></ul>	What do you have to find in this question? Is there a particular section where you should look for it?
2	<ul><li>Work your way through the text line by line looking carefully, so you do not miss points.</li><li>Underline or highlight each point you find as you go.</li></ul>	Read the extracts carefully to find the ten items. For example, in the second text you will immediately find 'The banana is healthy' and this is one reason bananas are so popular.
3	<ul><li>Check you have found the number of points you need.</li><li>Often you can copy out a detail from the text, but make sure the point makes complete sense.</li></ul>	Now check the rest of the points and note down your answers. For example, from the last paragraph of the first extract, you could say 'Bananas are "packed with energy, fibre and vitamins"'.

BRITAIN has gone bananas. Over the past 12 months we have consumed an unprecedented 3.5 billion pieces of the tropical fruit, forcing our native apple into a poor second place.

The nation's banana boom is one of the most remarkable nutritional phenomena of recent years, a guide not just to the flowering health consciousness of the British people but also to the country's economic health.

We spend more money on bananas than any other supermarket item apart from petrol and lottery tickets, and more than 95 per cent of our households buy them every week. Bananas are us, it seems.

The addiction will be reinforced this week as TV viewers watch endless Wimbledon shots of tennis players munching their way through hundreds of bananas, a fruit that is now considered to be indispensable for recovery between sets and rallies.

Yet a century ago hardly anyone in Britain had tasted or even seen a banana. The first commercial refrigerated shipment arrived 100 years ago this month, triggering a national love affair from which we have never looked back.

A striking measure of the banana's popularity can be seen in trade figures that show sales in the UK rocketed by more than 150 per cent over the past 17 years, while fruit sales in general have risen by a mere 15 per cent.

Bananas have flourished at the expense of our own apples and pears. Last year alone there was a 9 per cent growth in British banana sales while homegrown fruit languished.

'The banana has everything going for it, so its popularity should not seem that surprising,' said Lyndsey Morgan of the fruit's marketing organisation, the Banana Group.

'It is easy to open; it is packed with energy, fibre and vitamins; it is rich in potassium and low in calories. It is also a first-class hangover cure, stabilises blood pressure and soothes heartburn. And when you want to start weaning babies, mashed banana is the perfect food. You can even use the skins as garden fertiliser when you have finished. It is astonishingly versatile.'

Bananas provide sporting bonus

The banana is healthy, the ideal snack food if fitness is a priority. It is suggested that eating two bananas provides enough energy for a strenuous 90-minute workout.

The entire Manchester United team are said to eat banana and jam sandwiches before games, relying on the fruit to maintain their sporting prowess.

Examiner tips

- If you are asked to 'make a list' or 'list...' then you should do exactly that.
- If you are asked for ten points, include 11 or 12 if you can. You may have got something wrong or made the same point twice, but an extra point or two gives you a safety net.

Here are two student responses to the exam task below. Read the answers and the examiner comments.

List ten separate things mentioned in the two extracts, which help explain why bananas are so popular. [10]

Student 1

Ten separate things mentioned which help to explain why bananas are so popular are because we see celebrities eating them like the Manchester United football team. ✓ They also provide us with a lot of energy. ✓ They are also packed with fibre ✓ and with vitamins. ✓ Fibre is good for the muscles and tissues and vitamins are good for your teeth and bones, and for those on a low calorie diet they are really good because they don't have many calories in them. ✓ They are also an ideal snack ✓ as they are healthy ✓ and all kids love them. You can tell they are so popular as 'over 95 per cent of our households buy them every week'. There has also been an increase in the amount of bananas being sold. 'The nation's banana boom is one of the most remarkable of recent years.'

Examiner comments

- The student has not followed the instruction to *list* the points, it becomes hard for the student to check how many points have been made in the answer. Writing an answer in prose to this kind of question can take up more time than it needs to.
- This answer misses some easy marks that are available.
- It also gives information that is not asked for – there is nothing in the text about teeth and bones or that 'kids love them'. Always stick to the text.
- The final part of the answer drifts away from the question and there are no marks at all for the final three sentences.

'List or find' questions: how to improve your response

To improve your response you need to keep the question clearly in mind. In this question you were looking for things that explained why bananas are so popular. You can see from the student answers that you need to be thorough and methodical. You must find at least ten examples.

- The first answer made a number of points but because it was in full sentences the candidate probably spent more time on the question than was necessary.
- The second answer showed that the student knew exactly how to tackle the question and comfortably gained full marks. Each point was carefully separated and there was a clear focus on the question. Working in this way can help you feel confident about tackling the rest of the paper. You know you have got off to a really good start.

Student 2

- Wimbledon tennis players eat lots of them, so lots of people watching TV will want to do the same. ✓
- They are easy to open. ✓
- They are packed with energy. ✓
- They have lots of fibre. ✓
- They are rich in potassium. ✓
- They are low in calories. ✓
- Bananas are healthy. ✓
- They are an ideal snack food. ✓
- The banana is good for fitness – helps to keep you fit. ✓
- Eating two bananas gives enough energy for a tough 90-minute workout. ✓
- Lots of sportsmen eat them (the Man Utd team) before games to maintain their sporting prowess. ✓

Examiner comments

- This is a very good answer. The student has tracked through the text methodically and missed nothing.
- In places there are little bits of explanation to make sure the point is clearly made. Eleven points have been made, so even if one of the points were to have been wrong, the answer would still have gained a good mark.

Peer/Self-assessment activity

1 Which response is your answer closest to?

2 Note down any points you missed, which could have earned you a mark.

3 Did you make any points that did not earn you a mark?

4 How could you improve next time?

Putting it into practice

On your own or with a partner explain what you now know about:
- finding relevant points in a text
- what makes the difference between a weak answer and a typical Grade C answer – look carefully at the two examples and the examiner comments.

In the future:
- you can practise this skill with several of the texts you come across
- give yourself 12–13 minutes to practise this skill.

Your learning

This lesson will help you to:

- practise selecting relevant details
- develop a secure approach to 'list and find' questions.

'List or find' questions ask you to find relevant details. Make sure you list enough points. Check the question if you are unsure.

Activity 1

Read the website brochure and answer the question below.

List ten outdoor activities mentioned in the brochure that are available at Astley Woods. [10]

Examiner tips

- Be methodical, relevant and thorough.
- Remember that your bullet points should make sense.

Astley Woods 'Action Plus' Holidays

Why choose an Astley Woods 'Action Plus' Holiday? Maybe you want a holiday that pushes you to the limit. Or you have children who enjoy trying their hand at new, exciting activities. An 'Action Plus' holiday delivers excitement and challenge for all. But if you would rather enjoy more gentle pursuits in locations of wonderful natural beauty, Astley Woods holiday centres can offer that too. Enjoy the breeze when you sail across the lake, or join one of our woodland walks with our friendly Tracker Guides. And if you are looking for more challenge, you could always try the Log Swing, the High Tree Trek or the Zip Wire Challenge.

Whatever you want from a holiday, Astley Woods works tirelessly to offer 'Action Plus' holidays that will leave you with the warm glow of personal achievement and of time well spent in beautiful natural surroundings.

Astley Woods also provides superb accommodation for your holiday. We offer our standard 'Wychwood Forest' chalets for guests who simply want to enjoy the huge range of facilities available at our sites. For guests who want to be pampered, we offer our 'New Forest' chalets which are exclusively designed and stylishly furnished to the highest standards, and include en-suite bathrooms and saunas.

Children's 'Action Plus' Holidays

At Astley Woods we know that children learn best while they're having fun. That's why we have created a fantastic range of activities for children in every age group, and all of them are run by expert, qualified staff.

You can watch your children taking part in new activities, making new friends and learning new skills – and you are welcome to join in as much, or as little, as you'd like to. Or you can have some well-earned time to yourself, knowing that your children are in the safe, dependable hands of our staff.

Astley Woods Family Holidays

With their location, in 300 acres of unspoilt natural forest, the Astley Woods holiday centres offer a great choice of outdoor activities for all the family and for groups of all ages. We have something for everyone: from horse-riding to archery and from bird-watching to canoeing. Our instructors are all highly qualified and will help build your confidence and skill, whether you're an expert or beginner, ensuring your enjoyment whatever activity you choose.

We know that after a day spent exploring, playing or just relaxing, you'll want to enjoy a family meal together. We offer a range of superb restaurants and bistros where you can do just that, re-living the experiences of the day in a relaxed atmosphere. Each of our centres has a variety of themed restaurants, and with menus from every continent, we're sure that you'll feel spoilt for choice.

Memories to hold forever

Can you remember your own family holidays as a child: carefree, full of fun and memories that last forever? Let us help to create those experiences for all the family. The stunning forest locations and the magic of nature become the backdrop for family memories that will last a lifetime.

A Children's 'Action Plus' holiday will give all the family the opportunity to spend precious time together, as well as offering your children a range of supervised activities that will mean they'll never get bored the whole time they're with us. We also make sure that whilst they are enjoying themselves, you can have time for yourself, either to make the most of the facilities on offer, or to just relax in the delightful surroundings.

Whether it's inside or outdoors, your children will have plenty of activities to choose from. Outside, they can enjoy the soccer schools, abseiling and paintballing, whilst inside there are activities like fashion-design, movie-making and DJing. Every age and interest is catered for and because our emphasis is firmly on safety and on fun, you can be sure that you can relax when they are letting off steam.

There's so much more to keep them entertained at Astley Woods holiday centres than they could ever manage to do in just a single visit, so they're sure to pester you for another visit. We hope you'll share their wish to return again and again.

Activity 2

In this activity, you are asked to tackle two, five-mark questions, but the process is exactly the same. Read the newspaper article and answer the questions below.

1 **Look at the first five paragraphs (down to 'achieve something with our lives').**
   Tim Siadatan says, 'Jamie has managed to completely change nine people's lives'. List five details from the text which show how life has changed for the trainee chefs. [5]

2 **Look at the rest of the text.**
   List five problems Jamie Oliver faced during the training scheme. [5]

How Jamie saved me, by new-born chef

When he was a young boy, Tim Siadatan, one of 14 children, had to work for four days a week after school to raise money to buy himself new clothes.

Today, after graduating as one of the final nine teenagers who survived Jamie Oliver's crash course in running a restaurant, Siadatan is planning to open his own chain of diners one day. 'Jamie has managed to completely change nine people's lives overnight,' he told *The Observer* in his first interview. 'What he has done is amazing; he's taught us that with passion and determination you can get any career you want and be a success; a real, heavy-duty success.' Siadatan, 19, was one of 15 young people picked by Oliver from 15,000 jobless hopefuls earlier this year to be filmed learning to cook in his new London restaurant, Fifteen.

The resulting Channel 4 programme, *Jamie's Kitchen*, won record viewing figures as more than six million people tuned in over five weeks to watch the often painful learning curve as the unemployed youngsters gradually transformed themselves into efficient semi-professionals.

Now *Jamie's Kitchen* is finished, the real work is getting under way, with the young chefs working 18-hour days, six days a week to satisfy the hordes of diners eager to test their new proficiency.

'Some of us joined this scheme as naive, narrow kids,' said Siadatan. 'We have been transformed into incredibly focused, career-minded young people. Oliver has given us passion for a career and has instilled love for it in us. I love going to work, and how many people can say that? We now all believe we can achieve something with our lives.'

Viewers watched in incredulity as the students appeared to rebel against 27-year-old Oliver's attempts to cajole them into working, opting instead to accuse him of using them to forward his own career and often not turning up for work at all.

That version of events was not, however, Siadatan claimed, the full story. 'The way they portrayed us was a bit sneaky,' he said. 'They indicated we were all complete down-and-outs, which really wasn't the case at all.

Examiner tips

- Remember these questions are asking for lists, so either number your answers or put them in bullet points.
- Be methodical and thorough. Check that every point answers the question.
- Try to find a sixth point for each question if you can.

Peer/Self-assessment activity

1 Check your answers to Activities 1 and 2.
  - Did you find enough clear points?
  - Did you present and organise your answer in the appropriate way?

2 Now try to mark your answers to Activities 1 and 2.

3 Where are your strengths? Where is your answer not so strong? Make a list of one or two things you need to improve and practise these skills.

I know the producers had to do their job, but the programme portrayed us in a way that means the average person thinks we're ungrateful little slobs who never turned up on time and never worked hard enough. I don't care though,' he added. 'Jamie knows the truth, and my friends and family know what really went on.'

Siadatan admitted, however, that there were serious problems with three students thrown off the course just days before the restaurant was due to open after failing to turn up at the swish London restaurants at which Oliver had arranged work experience.

'These people were giving him so much trouble the rest of us couldn't believe it,' he said. 'It was awful.'

There were not just problems with the students; until just days before the scheduled launch date, the restaurant looked like a building site. 'We really thought it wasn't going to be open on time,' admitted Siadatan. 'It was devastating; for about four days, we thought the whole thing was going to collapse.'

Oliver was, Siadatan said, supportive throughout. 'Jamie kept reassuring us that he wouldn't turn his back on us and we believed him. He wasn't getting any sleep and it was his money on the line, but he kept it together just to keep the rest of us going. He sent us back to work at other restaurants, then people began not turning up again,' he said. 'That was unbelievable when Jamie was going through so much himself.' A deep affection has developed between the remaining nine students: 'I call them my London family,' said Siadatan. 'We're just like brothers and sisters.'

But although Siadatan's period as Oliver's student will end at the beginning of next summer, the youngsters will not be left on their own. Instead, Cheeky Chops, the charity formed by Oliver, will award each new-born chef a scholarship to set up on their own and supply them with the help and contacts they need.

'Jamie said he would always be there for us, and we know he will be,' said Siadatan. 'That's a fabulous feeling to have.'

'Find specific information' questions

Your learning

This lesson will help you to:

- select relevant details from a passage
- present the information clearly.

'Find specific information' questions ask you to find specific details in the text.

- You need to work through the whole text in a methodical way.
- The texts used are often leaflets or brochures.
- There are usually a number of parts to the question. Make sure you do not miss any.

Activity 1

Read the text opposite and answer the questions below. The text is a leaflet from the Royal National Lifeboat Institution (RNLI), which is encouraging readers to donate money to the charity.

1 **Give five examples of the very difficult conditions that lifeboat crews often have to work in. [5]**

2 **How much funding does the RNLI receive from the British government? [I]**

3 **On average, how many people are rescued by the RNLI:**
   - **each day [I]**
   - **each year? [I]**

4 **How much does it cost to provide a crew member with all of their protective gear? [I]**

5 **If you support the RNLI with an annual donation, what will you receive in return? [I]**

Examiner tips

- You will gain a mark for each correct detail.
- There is no need to put the information into sentences.
- Although you are searching for particular details, you will often be asked to group the details into a list.
- Read the question carefully to make sure you know exactly what details you have to find.

He'll face 10m waves, blizzards, Force 9 gales and sub-zero temperatures

Photography: Harriet Logan Graham Durrant: Inshore lifeboat Crew Member, Great Yarmouth and Gorleston lifeboat station

All we ask of you is £20

How your support helps the lifeboat service

For 186 years the RNLI's lifeboat crews have been going to sea to save lives. Today, as in 1824, our lifeboat service receives no UK Government funding. That's why your donations are so vital to us. Without your help, there simply wouldn't be a lifeboat service. Our volunteer crews are unpaid and risk their lives to save others. They rescue on average 21 people every day. As we are responding to an ever growing need, providing the very best equipment and training is the least we can do.

What your £20 could do

A gift of £20 can be incredibly useful. It can keep a lifeboat running for 5 minutes – which could be the difference between life and death for a seafarer. £20 could also go towards a pair of custom-made sea boots, designed to keep crew members sure-footed in rough conditions. And if just 50 people gave £20, we could kit out a crew member in protective gear, which costs approximately £1,000 per person. With more than 230 lifeboat stations around the United Kingdom and the Republic of Ireland, it's a huge task. So we're grateful for everything we receive.

The people who never count the cost to themselves

Our volunteers give amazing amounts of skill, courage and time. They give these selflessly and they rescue on average 7,500 people a year. Sailors, fishermen, children, mothers, wives, husbands and fathers all over the UK owe their lives to our crews.

Photo: Nigel Millard

Our crews face the toughest conditions.

They are prepared to go to sea in terrifying conditions – sometimes in total darkness and are on call 24 hours a day, 365 days a year. In fact, by the time you read this, an RNLI crew member may have rescued someone. But they can't do it without your help.

Help us today

Please support this appeal, and give £20, or whatever you can afford. If you're able to donate on an annual basis, in return we'll send you regular copies of *Lifeline*, our quarterly newsletter. It's full of news and rescue stories.

Thank you.
Tel: 0845 121 4999
or visit
rnli.org.uk/donation
The RNLI is the charity that saves lives at sea

Here are two student responses to the exam task below. Read the answers and the examiner comments.

Read the text and the exam questions below. The text is a leaflet from the Royal National Lifeboat Institution (RNLI), which is encouraging readers to donate money to the charity. [10]

1 Give five examples of the very difficult conditions that lifeboat crews often have to work in. [5]
2 How much funding does the RNLI receive from the British government? [1]
3 On average, how many people are rescued by the RNLI:
  ● each day [1]
  ● each year? [1]
4 How much does it cost to provide a crew member with all of their protective gear? [1]
5 If you support the RNLI with an annual donation, what will you receive in return? [1]

Extract typical of a F grade answer

Student 1

1 The difficult conditions the lifeboat crews have to face are blizzards,✓ Force 9 gales✓ and sub-zero temperatures.✓
2 The government give £1000 per person a year.✗
3 (a) 21 people ✓
  (b) – ✗
4 £20✗
5 An annual donation can keep a lifeboat running for 5 minutes or go towards a pair of sea boots.✗

Examiner comments

This answer shows the danger of not reading carefully enough.
● Question 1 is worth five marks but this response only identifies three points.
● Question 2 shows the importance of reading the question carefully.
● The second part of question 3 has not been attempted, but the answer is easy to locate. This student just needs to read all of the text carefully.
● In looking at the answers to questions 4 and 5 it is clear that the student has not read the questions carefully enough. In question 5, the words 'annual donation' have been noted but the student has not checked to see *exactly* what the question is asking.

Student 2

1 The lifeboat crews face: 1 10m waves. ✓ 2 Blizzards. ✓
   3 Force 9 gales. ✓ 4 Sub-zero temperatures. ✓
   5 Working in total darkness. ✓
2 They receive no funding ✓ from the government.
3 (a) On average 21 people ✓ are rescued every day.
   (b) On average 7,500 people ✓ are rescued each year.
4 It costs £1000 ✓ to kit out a crew member with
   protective gear.
5 People who donate money annually receive 'Lifeline', ✓ the
   quarterly RNLI newsletter.

Examiner comments

- This candidate knows exactly what to do and has read the leaflet carefully.
- There are no mistakes and every answer is clear and well focused on the question.
- This answer would gain full marks.

'Finding specific information' questions: how to improve your response

To improve your response you need to keep the question clearly in mind. In these questions you need to look for very specific details. You can see from the student answers that you need to be careful and keep the question in mind when you answer.

- The first answer shows the danger of not reading carefully and silly errors cost the student important marks.
- The second answer was exactly how this kind of question should be answered. You do not need long 'wordy' answers because you are looking for very specific details.
- When you read the question, it may be helpful to highlight or underline what you have to do (for example, give <u>five</u> examples) or exactly what you are looking for (for example, <u>each day</u>, <u>each year</u>).

Putting it into practice

On your own or with a partner explain what you now know about:

- finding specific details in a text
- how to check you are looking for exactly the right details.

In the future:

- you can practise this skill with several texts you come across
- give yourself 12–13 minutes to practise this skill.

Peer/Self-assessment activity

1 Which response is your answer closest to?

2 Note down any points you missed that could have earned you a mark.

3 Did you make any points that did not earn you a mark?

4 How could you improve next time?

Your learning

This lesson will help you to:

- practise finding specific information
- develop a secure approach to this type of question.

When answering 'finding specific information' questions remember to:
- answer each part of the question
- read the text methodically
- find the specific details you need.

Activity 1

Read the text opposite and answer the questions below. The text is from a brochure that is trying to encourage people to visit Bradford.

1 List three of Bradford's historic buildings. [3]

2 List two theatres in Bradford. [2]

3 List two of the sports facilities in Bradford. [2]

4 List three film festivals that take place in Bradford each year. [3]

BRADFORD

From stunning Victorian architecture to an amazing 3D visual feast at the IMAX Cinema, Bradford is culturally rich with a city centre full of history, yet vibrant and cosmopolitan. Two hundred years ago Bradford changed from a small rural town, whose people spun wool and wove cloth, into the wool capital of the world. Bradford now enjoys a fantastic architectural legacy from this period, a heritage that can be explored through a series of self guided trails available from the Tourist Information Centre.

Many exceptional historic buildings remain, including the Grade 1 listed City Hall (built 1873), the gothic style Wool Exchange (1867), and the 15th century cathedral. Bradford's history is evident in the popular Bradford Industrial Museum in the unique commercial area known as Little Germany.

There are plenty of modern attractions to capture the imagination.

The award winning National Media Museum – five floors of interactive displays – charts the past, present and future of image making and has three cinemas, including the incredible IMAX experience with its giant 3D screen.

Other major attractions within the city include Cartwright Hall Art Gallery, set in beautiful Lister Park, voted Britain's best park in 2006; the Alhambra Theatre; and The Priestley Theatre. There is a packed programme of festivals and events, including three major film festivals and the world-famous Bradford Festival – two weeks of music, theatre, film and street events.

Those who prefer shopping will also love Bradford, as the city is home to a host of unusual speciality shops, markets and mill shops where many bargains can be found. In the city, high street names rub shoulders with local shops, and for an elegant upmarket shopping excursion outside the city, nearby Ilkley offers top quality shops from high fashion to fine chocolatiers.

The city's nightlife, with its rich variety of restaurants, bars and nightclubs, might surprise you. And discover for yourself why Bradford has been crowned UK Curry capital, with well over 200 Asian restaurants across the district. But Bradford also has an interesting mix of fine international cuisine and traditional Yorkshire fare. The city has many traditional pubs to enjoy, like the New Beehive Inn with its Edwardian interior and gas lit bars, which caters for the Real Ale enthusiast, and appears regularly in the Good Beer Guide.

Plus ...

In June, Bradford swings to the sounds of the festival with live music in Centenary Square. By night, take in a show at the magnificent Alhambra Theatre.

The Industrial Museum gears up daily for a public demonstration of its Motive Power engines at 10.30 am and 2.00 pm (most days).

Odsal Stadium is home to Rugby League's 2005 Super League champions, Bradford Bulls, while football takes centre stage across town at Valley Parade, the home of Bradford City. There's fun for all the family at Bradford's 11 public swimming pools, and some of the other sports facilities include ten-pin bowling in the city centre and ice skating at the ever-popular Bradford Ice Arena.

The National Media Museum has three diverse film festivals each year – The Bradford Film Festival (March), 'Bite the Mango' Film Festival (Sept) and The Bradford Animation Festival (Oct/Nov) – perfect for film lovers of all ages!

Peer/Self-assessment activity

1 Check your answer to Activity I.
   - Did you give the right number of details for each question (three historic buildings, two theatres and so on)?
   - Did you list the details so that the answer was clear and precise?

2 Now try to mark your answer to Activity I.

3 Where are your strengths? Where is your answer not so strong? Work with a partner. Each create a list of five questions about further details in the text. Test each other and improve your skills.

'Evidence' questions

If you are asked to find evidence, you need to:

- read the question carefully – notice the key words
- work through the whole text in a methodical way.

You may be asked a question such as the one below.

What evidence is there that the lifeboat crew were faced with a difficult rescue? [10]

Or you may be asked a question where the word 'evidence' does not appear in the question, for example the following.

What did Robert Lindsay enjoy about going to Center Parcs? [10]

This question is really asking you to provide the evidence from the article that the writer had an enjoyable time. You need to select and organise the evidence from the text. The more evidence you can provide, the higher your mark will be.

Activity 1

Read the article opposite and answer the question below.

What did Robert Lindsay enjoy about going to Center Parcs? [10]

- Key pieces of evidence have been underlined. These show you how to work on a passage and make a good selection of relevant details. You may be able to find other, equally important, details as well.
- Although quoting the text may be useful, in some cases you will need to explain the evidence a little. Sometimes it is easier to paraphrase – to put things in your own words.

Use the text to produce an answer. Practise ways of answering the question, including use of a few quotations. You should take no more than 12–13 minutes to complete this task.

FAMILY FUN AT CENTER PARCS

THERE are no stresses, just the welcome strain of working your way through a huge array of adult and child-friendly activities. A Center Parcs stay is a revelation, says actor Robert Lindsay.

The problem with being a parent is kids! I know I'm sounding like that cantankerous father Ben Harper, whom I play in BBC comedy *My Family*, but I have to model him on someone. Now don't get me wrong, I love my kids, but come on – I've got a life, they've got a life, we all have. So let's try to meet halfway.

We found the perfect happy medium at Center Parcs. I had a short break in my filming schedule that coincided with half-term for Sam, eight, and five-year-old Jamie, so we decided to give one a go. My 19-year-old daughter had been with friends years ago and really enjoyed it. Elveden Forest in Suffolk wasn't the nearest Parc to the family home in London but we like to have a bit of a drive when we're going away.

The overwhelming positive for me as we arrived was the lack of cars. I hate cars, even though I drive one. At the Parc they have a big parking area concealed by bushes. Vehicles disappear for the duration of your stay, while you use bikes to get around. No traffic! What a stress-beater.

Our 'executive' lodge was one that has been restyled by award-winning designer Tara Bernerd. It was a home away from home with cool furnishings and wall-mounted plasma TV, a nice forest view and even a sauna. The kids went crazy when they saw where we were staying; there was bags of space, an open fire and even a table that converted into a pool table.

The first thing my wife Rosie and I did was go for a massage in the spa lodge, which was fantastic. We then did an exploration, locating the huge main arena, housing everything from indoor swimming pool to cinema, where we picked up our bikes for the stay. The arena proved to be about a 10-minute gentle cycle away from our lodge.

Our stay was from a Thursday to a Sunday. In the mornings, we'd wander down to the shop to buy our food for breakfast, the only meal of the day we'd eat at the lodge. Then we'd depart for our different activities.

The boys would go to archery or quad-biking, for example, while I went fishing (I had to be taught again, it's been so long!). We'd then all get together to do something like sailing, which I love, on the Parc's lake.

The instructors were amazing. I don't know where they find them but they are superb. We'd either leave the boys with them, or stay and wait while they did their activities. There was always something for the adults to do as well, such as table tennis, rather than just hanging around.

You'll never have experienced such active days. Also on offer were such things as abseiling, rollerblading, badminton and bowling. After lunch we'd have a siesta and shower, before dressing for dinner – well, for a bike ride then dinner! There are just so many ways to busy yourself at Center Parcs and work up an appetite for a meal you'll feel you've really earned.

The restaurants cater for every taste. There were ones with their own wine lists and ones with child-friendly zones […]. I love Sunday brunch, from my time working in America, and there was a great restaurant for this, stocked with every Sunday newspaper.

One night we were given a cabaret – well, actually more of a full-blown show with a professional West End feel to it. Our food continued to be served as it played out. After dessert, there was a lovely nightcap for the two grown-ups, while the boys sat enthralled by the show.

I've always felt that this country hasn't really developed the mentality to deal with children and adults together, unlike such countries as France and Spain but Center Parcs has it spot-on.

It was an invigorating break, one that restored my confidence in holidaying in Britain with my children. Just a word of advice – if you're visiting during the school holidays, make sure you book activities in advance.

Will we go back? We use it all the time now – for a weekend break, or just to have a change of scene and get away from the domestic stresses and enjoy being with the kids!

Activity 2

Now read the article about a lifeboat rescue and answer the question below.

What evidence is there that the lifeboat crew were faced with a difficult rescue? [10]

Dramatic mid-Channel rescue in

heavy seas

Eight sailors from the cargo ship *Ice Prince* were taken on board the Torbay lifeboat late last night in a dramatic rescue, described by lifeboat coxswain, Mark Criddle, as a 'once in a lifetime' rescue. An emergency call had been put out by the captain of the *Ice Prince* when its cargo of timber shifted in the heavy seas and gale force winds and it began to list dangerously. The conditions were so bad that it took the lifeboat about one and three quarter hours to reach the stricken ship, stranded without power 33 miles off the south Devon coast. Criddle explained that although the first three sailors were taken off quickly, it had taken more than an hour to get the remaining five off, who were frightened to leave their ship and jump across to the safety of the lifeboat, because of the heavy swell running. He said the lifeboat had to make many attempts to get alongside the *Ice Prince*, with the lifeboat crew shouting encouragement to the sailors to jump to safety. However, some of the crew were very distressed and reluctant to leave their vessel.

The *Ice Prince* was 132 metres long, weighing 70,000 tonnes and made of steel, while the lifeboat was just 17 metres long and made of fibreglass. The challenge for the men on the lifeboat was taking a 17 metre lifeboat alongside such a large ship with a huge amount of cargo.

One minute the lifeboat would be right alongside the *Ice Prince* with the crew calling for the sailors to jump, the next minute the lifeboat found itself five metres below them in the heavy swell.

Some of the *Ice Prince* sailors really did not want to leave the ship for the tiny 41 tonne lifeboat that was pitching and rolling in the sea. One of the men on board the *Ice Prince* fell heavily into the sea, but the lifeboat crew managed to pull him on board. It was a difficult night's work because of the treacherous sea conditions and because there were no other lights apart from emergency lighting, as the *Ice Prince* had lost all power.

Second coxswain Roger Good was one of the lifeboat crew working hard to persuade the sailors to jump overboard and then pulling them to safety.

He said: 'I lost count of how many times we took the lifeboat into position to get them off. It's a very unnatural thing for them to have to do, to jump overboard in those conditions. It's a case of getting the lifeboat in as close as possible and getting them on the side of their boat, and then you grab hold of them and keep pulling and pull them on the deck. Any aching or cold hands don't matter; your adrenaline is running and you just grab hold of them, drag them to the boat and get that next one. It's only now you sit back and think, "Yes, that was really hard".'

Here are two student responses to the exam task below. Read the answers and the examiner comments.

What evidence is there that the lifeboat crew were faced with a difficult rescue? [10]

Extract typical of a E grade answer

Student 1

What made the rescue really difficult was that the conditions were awful.✓ Because of the waves the lifeboat kept on rolling back and forwards✓ so the sailors on the ship couldn't jump and be close enough to the lifeboat at the same time.

Also the sailors were frightened to leave the ship.✓ This took time to get them to jump overboard. Persuading the sailors to leave their ship also made the rescue more difficult✓ and when they finally jumped, the crew from the lifeboat had to grab a hold of the sailors and pull them aboard.✓ Also, trying to get the lifeboat exactly 17 metres away from the 'Ice Prince' proved very difficult.

Examiner comments

Strong point
- The student has included some evidence.

Weak points
- The answer is not very methodical in the approach to the text and some simple points are not included.
- Notice that the second point comes from the second paragraph but then the next point comes from the first paragraph. This takes up more time and means that points are missed.
- The final sentence of the answer shows some mis-reading. The candidate has confused the length of the lifeboat with the problems it had getting alongside the *Ice Prince*.

Student 2

The rescue was difficult because the conditions were bad and they had to travel a long way to even reach the ship. The report says there were 'heavy seas'✓ which would make the rescue hard and 'gale force winds'.✓ The ship had also begun to 'list dangerously'✓ so it might easily sink. The rescue took place 33 miles from the coast✓ and it had taken the lifeboat one and three quarter hours✓ to even reach the 'Ice Prince'. Another reason it was dangerous was because it was hard to get the lifeboat close to the ship in severe conditions.✓ They had to try to convince the sailors to jump off the 'Ice Prince' on to the lifeboat.✓ When the sailors jumped, they had to pull them on board in the severe weather conditions,✓ 'grab hold of them and keep pulling and pull them on the deck'.

Examiner comments

Strong points
- This answer shows a good focus on the question and there are lots of details that would be rewarded.
- It also tracks the text fairly methodically especially in the first paragraph.

Weak point
- There are some marks that this student did not pick up.

'Evidence' questions: how to improve your response

To improve your response you need to be completely focused on the question.
- It is helpful to highlight the key word in the question. Here the key words would be *evidence* and *difficult rescue*.
- Then you should work your way through the text highlighting or underlining the details. Remember, the more points you can find the better your chances of a high mark.
- Sometimes you may feel you need to explain things a little or it may be sensible to use short quotations. However, you must work methodically through the text.
- Aim to be as methodical as the answer given by Student 2.

Putting it into practice

On your own or with a partner explain what you now know about:
- finding evidence in a text
- using the text in your answer
- organising your answer
- including any necessary explanation
- what makes the difference between typical E grade and C grade responses.

In the future:
- practise this type of question with several texts
- get used to highlighting the text quickly and using what you have found
- practise including short quotations in your answer
- work towards producing a complete answer in 12–13 minutes.

> **Your learning**
>
> **This lesson will help you to:**
>
> - practise selecting relevant evidence
> - develop a secure approach to this type of question.

When answering 'Evidence' questions you need to work methodically through the text, underline or highlight the relevant points and use them neatly in your answer.

Activity 1

Read this extract and answer the question below.

What evidence does the writer of the article give to show that ASBOs are not effective? [10]

Anti-Social Behaviour Orders (ASBOs) were introduced in 1999 as part of the government's drive against anti-social behaviour. They are supposed to work by frightening the offender back into line, with the threat of a two-year prison sentence if ignored.

Thugs consider Asbos a 'diploma', says report

YOUNG THUGS consider Asbos a 'diploma' in offending which they can break repeatedly and with impunity, a devastating report reveals. The Youth Justice Board found half of all orders given to the teenage tearaways are breached – in some cases six times or more each – but most are simply let-off by the courts. Only six per cent were jailed for flouting their Asbo.

One judge told the report's authors that Young Offender Institutes were too full for the regime to be properly enforced. Instead, most are released with a curfew order or a conditional or absolute discharge.

Parents and carers of young people handed orders said they were viewed as a 'diploma' and boosted a child's street credibility.

'Some of the friends are left out now because they're not on an Asbo,' said the mother of three young men who were all on Asbos. 'I know a boy that's hell-bent on getting an Asbo because he feels left out.'

A district judge told researchers, who gave anonymity to those taking part, that youngsters who breached their orders were often not being properly punished. In a damning indictment of Labour's failure to provide enough prison places – for adults and children – he said: 'The danger is that you would increase the (prison) population enormously if we enforced Asbos fully. So I think there are quite a lot of people breaching orders and not a lot happening to them when they do.'

Analysis of 137 Asbo cases for the YJB found 47, or 49 per cent, had breached their order at least once. Of these, 42 – or 31 per cent – broke their conditions on more than one occasion. Among that group, six yobs breached their Asbo on six occasions or more.

But, when it came to punishments, custody was rare rather than the norm. This is despite the fact that even before getting an Asbo, half of children had three or more previous convictions. Some 77 per cent had a least one.

Of 18 punished where breaching their Asbo was the sole offences for which they were in court, only one was sent to a Young Offender Institute.

In the 49 cases where they were being punished for breaching their Asbo alongside another crime, only 18 were sent to custody.

The YJB, which last week called for fewer young criminals to be imprisoned because it had run out of detention spaces, said the answer was to issue fewer Asbos.

Peer/Self-assessment activity

1 Check your answers to Activity I.
   • Did you find enough clear points?
   • Did you present and organise your answer so that it followed the text line by line? For example, the first point you should have made was that the writer does not think ASBOs are effective because thugs think of them as 'diplomas': they are pleased when they are given them. This information comes in the heading and in the first sentence of the article.

2 Now try to mark your answer to Activity I.

3 Where are your strengths? Where is your answer not so strong? Make a list of one or two things you need to improve and practise these skills.

'Explain' questions

Your learning

This lesson will help you to:

- understand how to approach 'explain' questions
- explain what a text is saying at surface level and a deeper level.

In the Foundation Tier exam, 'Explain' questions often combine two parts. For example:

What did the writer's children enjoy about the visit to Warwick Castle? Why did they enjoy it? [10]

For the 'What' part of the question you need to select relevant information and details from the text (see page 34).

For the 'Why' part of the question you need to 'read between the lines'. You need to give a comment to show that you understand what the text is saying at a deeper level. This part of the question may start with 'Why' or 'How'.

Reading between the lines is a key reading skill called **inference**. There are many levels of understanding in most texts. You need to show that you understand the surface meaning. You also need to show you can see the deeper ideas the writer is trying to get across. This is inference.

Examiner tips

Inference is a key skill in aiming for a C grade.

For example, one candidate wrote in part of their answer:

This is a sensible inference about why they would like to hold the sword

A sensible selection of detail

The children had an opportunity to hold a medieval sword which they really liked. ✓ This would be exciting for them because it was a real sword ✓ and most people don't ever get to hold real weapons that could kill people. ✓ Also, holding a weapon from such a long time ago that might have actually been used in a battle would make them feel as though they were part of history. ✓

Offers another sensible inference about why they liked the sword

Another sensible inference that shows the candidate really trying to explore why the children liked the sword

Read the text below and answer the question on page 34.
The extract is from an article written about a visit to Warwick Castle.

Once inside the castle, signs pointed us to each of the major exhibitions and displays. The children, being children, immediately picked the dungeons and torture chambers as the first place to visit.

A guide dressed as a knight, complete with a very realistic sword, greeted us and at once got the children in the mood by warning Amy that the Winnie the Pooh character on her rucksack might be afraid of the dungeons. We then had to follow the tiny stone steps down into the darkness and it was not hard to make the children realise that this was one place that visitors in medieval times would not have liked to come! Back in the daylight, Amy found it most amusing that the stocks and the rack were used as methods of torture – until one of the guides explained that prisoners' guts used to burst open when they were stretched as far as they could go. Why is it kids always love gruesome stories?

Our next move was to the armoury and I was delighted to see there were now plenty of interactive displays for the kids, including a television and video presentation and a series of wooden chests which asked questions and then had to be opened to find the answers.

There was also a chance to hold a real medieval sword, which amazed the girls when we told them the knights would have run into battle carrying them. Olivia loved the sword and instantly asked to try on a soldier's helmet. Amy, meanwhile, was fascinated by a display of muskets and duelling pistols, which she said looked very different from the guns in today's films.

Back outside again and the Bowman of Warwick was on hand to teach us how to use a bow and arrow. Then it was into the Great Hall to see the luxurious furniture and wall hangings which made the castle a home in times gone by. The girls then spent an hour trying on medieval and Victorian costumes.

Our final visit was to the Kingmaker exhibition where the wax models depicted life in the days when a king ruled the country and peasants worked the land. The sights, sounds and smells of the exhibition brought it all to life and the wax figures were so real they actually gave us all the creeps. When a wax horse neighed and moved its tail, I admit I jumped higher than the children!

Activity 1

Now use the following steps to answer the question below:

What did the writer's children enjoy about the visit to Warwick Castle? Why did they enjoy it? [10]

First, plan your answer. You might find it useful to use a table like the one below to do this.

What they enjoyed on the visit (evidence from the text)	Why they enjoyed the visit (your comments or inferences)
They wanted to go straight to the dungeons and torture chamber. They 'immediately picked the dungeons and torture chambers as the first place to visit'.	Children would be fascinated and excited by the chance to see a real dungeon and torture chamber, especially as the dark would make it realistic and spooky.
They liked the guide who was dressed as a knight, he 'got the children in the mood'.	A guide dressed up would have made the experience more realistic for children.
Amy was amused by the tales of prisoners being tortured. She liked the 'gruesome stories'.	Children like to hear horrible stories of torture.

1 Look through the text for key details that show **what** the children enjoyed. Fill in the first column of your table. Include some quotations to provide evidence that supports the details. This will be rewarded by an examiner.

2 Now look through the text to see **why** the children enjoyed their visit. Fill in the second column of your table, providing evidence where possible.

Examiner tips

● Although the question may be in two parts, the best way of tackling it is to give a detail from the text and then offer a comment alongside it.
● Stay in sequence and track the text carefully. Highlight the key details or short quotations in the text. Use these details or quotations for the 'What' part of the question.
● As you go along, link the above with a comment that explains 'Why' or 'How'. Weaving your comments into the answer in this way will mean that by the end of your work, you will have made a number of different comments and gained more marks.

Activity 2

Finally, use the evidence and comments from your table to build an answer.
Remember, in the exam your answer must be in continuous prose.

Practise combining the 'What' and the 'Why' into sentences to answer the question.
Your answer might begin:

> The first thing the children enjoyed was a trip
> to the dungeon and torture chamber, which they
> would have enjoyed because children would always
> be excited to see a real dungeon and the darkness
> would have made it realistic and spooky...

GradeStudio

Check your answer

- Did you find enough evidence from the text?
- Did you manage to say something about the evidence you found?
- Did your answer link evidence and comment well?

Here are two student responses to the exam task below. Read the answers and the examiner comments.

What did the writer's children enjoy about the visit to Warwick Castle? Why did they enjoy it? [10]

Student 1

The writer's children enjoyed the dungeons and torture chamber✓ and Amy would have like the way the guide said that the Winnie the Pooh character on her rucksack would be scared of the dungeons. ✓
When they went into the armoury they could enjoy the interactive displays that included wooden chests which asked question and then had to be opened to find the answers. ✓
Also they liked the experience of holding a real medieval sword✓ and trying on the medieval and Victorian costumes. ✓ In the kingmaker exhibition which had wax models of royalty and peasants, the wax models were so life-like it was almost scary, so they enjoyed that. ✓ Overall, the writer's children enjoyed themselves immensely.

Examiner comments

Student I selects some details of what the children enjoyed but never attempts to explain *why* they enjoyed themselves. The student has not been able to show the skill of inference in the answer and so it limits the mark that can be given.

'Explain' questions: how to improve your response

To improve your response you need to show that you have understood what is being said in the text and to keep a clear focus on the question.

- In this question you were asked to explain **what** the children enjoyed about their visit. You needed to show the skill of inference by making sensible comments, based on the evidence, about **why** they enjoyed it, for example having the chance to hold a medieval sword.
- The first answer used the text well to select evidence but does not attempt to explain *why* the children enjoyed their time.
- The second answer shows you how to link comments with the evidence or detail from the text. It is quite thorough in its use of the text and there is a deliberate attempt to give a viewpoint. Notice that a number of sentences begin 'I think...', which introduces a reason why the children enjoyed the visit. This is the structure you need to use with this type of question.

Student 2

The article states that the children wanted to go straight to the dungeon✓ and they would have enjoyed until the guide told them horrible stories of what happened there. I think they enjoyed the dungeons because children from this day and age will only have read about methods of torturing so will have been fascinated by seeing the real thing.✓ The article also says that the girls are 'amazed' when they are shown the sword✓ and told about it. I think they enjoyed being allowed to hold a weapon from so long ago and it might have been used in a real battle.✓ We are told that Amy was 'fascinated' by some of the displays of guns✓ and Olivia wanted to try on a soldier's helmet,✓ so they must have enjoyed both of these things. Lastly we are told the girls enjoyed dressing up in all the Victorian costumes.✓ I think this is because they were a lot different from the clothes worn today.✓

Examiner comments

This answer uses the evidence well but it also tries to add some explanation about why the children enjoyed the visit. Notice how the student works quite methodically through the text, and usually links the details of what they enjoy with a reason why. There are some easy points that are missed such as the interactive displays and the realistic wax figures that made them jump but this is a good attempt.

Putting it into practice

On your own or with a partner explain what you now know about:

- using evidence from the text to show you have understood what you have read
- linking the evidence to comments (or inferences) that show your understanding
- what makes the difference between typical E and C grade responses.

In the future:

- make sure you practise this skill using a variety of texts
- try to link evidence from the text to inferences
- aim to produce complete answers in 12–13 minutes.

Peer/Self-assessment activity

1 Which response is your answer closest to?

2 What evidence and inferences has each student used in their answer?

3 Note down any evidence or inferences you missed that could have earned you a mark.

4 How could you improve next time?

Your learning

This lesson will help you to:

- practise combining evidence and inference
- develop a secure approach to 'explain' questions.

When answering 'Explain' questions, remember to do the following.

- Make comments that are focused on the key words of the question. In the example below your comments must be on the **changes** that have occurred.
- Use the key words in the question to begin some of your sentences. For example, you could begin: 'One of the main changes that has happened on our streets is…'.
- Look for the relevant evidence from the text to support or prove what you are saying.
- In a question like the one below, try to link the two parts of the question. Here, you should explain the change and then follow it up with some explanation of why this is a concern.

Activity 1

Read this extract from a newspaper article and answer the question below.

Explain what have been the main changes that have happened on our streets, according to this newspaper article. Why are the changes seen as a concern? [10]

Half of children NEVER go out to play in the street

Britain's streets have become 'no-go areas' for children with almost half of five to ten-year-olds never playing outside their homes, a report shows today.

Two generations ago, it was rare for youngsters not to play on the street, with many doing so every day, a survey found.

Now, fast-moving traffic and parents' worries over paedophiles have destroyed neighbourhood relations and robbed areas of their community spirit, research by the Living Streets charity claims.

Its report, No ball games here (or shopping, playing or talking to the neighbours), shows how communities have changed as car use has mushroomed and planning decisions failed to promote walking.

The survey of more than 1,000 parents and pensioners found that childhood was increasingly marked by shrinking freedom and greater adult supervision with 49 per cent of youngsters now never playing in the street. In contrast, just 12 per cent of over-65s said they had never played outside their homes when they were young while 47 per cent said they did so every day.

Even the percentage of today's parents playing out as children was far bigger than it is now, suggesting that changes in the past 20 years are responsible for the decline. Youngsters are also less likely to walk to school, contributing to childhood obesity and denying them opportunities to extend their social networks.

- Read the text carefully to find information about the changes that have happened on our streets.
- Then look carefully through the text to see why these changes are causing concern.
- When you are practising work for the exam, use a table to help you to link the changes with the concerns. This will help you to organise your material. However, in the exam itself you should always answer in sentences rather than in bullet points or in the form of a table, unless the question tells you to organise your answer in this way.
- Make sure that your answer is as clear and precise as you can make it.

Part of the problem is an exaggerated fear among parents their children would be abducted, when in fact youngsters are no more likely to be snatched today than 30 years ago.

'Playing freely on the street strengthens friendships, keeps children healthy and helps them to cope with risky situations, but the opportunities for children to do so have been falling rapidly,' the report said.

Meanwhile, more than a quarter of residents with young families know fewer than two neighbours well enough to have a conversation with.

This is in contrast to over-65s, who said that when they were young parents, they knew at least five neighbours well enough to have a conversation with them.

Parents are also now less likely to shop locally. Two thirds drive to out-of-town stores – a reversal of the position the generation before when most went to shops within walking distance with one in five going to specialist stores like butchers.

Just two per cent of 30 to 40-year-olds use local specialist shops. These trends had 'ripped the heart from many of our towns', the report said.

Peer/Self-assessment activity

1 Check your answers to Activity I.
- Did you follow the text in a clear sequence?
- Did you use evidence from the text?
- Were you able to link the concerns to the details?
- Did you make the main points clear?
- Did you keep quotations short and integrate them into your answer?
- Did you use your own words to make inferences?
- Did you choose your words carefully?
- Did you have an overall sense of the writer's argument?

2 Now try to mark your answer to Activity I. Use the mark scheme below to help you.

⊕ Improve your learning

8–10 marks
▶ Selects and organises a range of points well.
▶ Answers show good links between the two parts of the question.

5–7 marks
▶ Spots a range of details.
▶ Better answers begin to link concerns with details.

3–4 marks
▶ Collects a few of the details about changes on Britain's streets.
▶ Struggles to link the concerns with the details.

Your learning

This lesson will help you to:

- understand how texts attempt to present an impression of their subject
- learn how to approach this type of question.

Sometimes a question is asked in the Reading paper about what **impression** an article or a factsheet creates of a place, an individual, group of people or an organisation. This simply means the kind of view you might have of a place, person or organisation when you read what is being said about it or them. For example, if someone is described as 'lively', you may think they would be fun to know.

Activity 1

Read the passage opposite. It was written by Bill Bryson after he had visited Weston-super-Mare. When you read the passage, it becomes clear that he is trying to create a particular impression of the town, and does this by the careful choice of words and phrases. Notice that all of the details he chooses to write about add to the impression you get of the town.

1. What impressions do you think the writer wanted the reader to have of the town?

2. List any words or phrases that help to create these impressions. For example, Bryson says the streets were 'empty, dark and full of slanting rain', which suggests how he felt about his visit to the town.

It was only a little after six when I stepped from the Exeter train and ventured into the town, but already the whole of Weston appeared to be indoors beyond drawn curtains. The streets were empty, dark and full of slanting rain. I walked from the station through a concrete shopping precinct and out on to the front where a black unseen sea made restless whooshing noises. Most of the hotels along the front were dark and empty, and the few that were open didn't look particularly enticing. I walked a mile or so to a cluster of three brightly lit establishments and selected a place called the Birchfield. It was fairly basic, but clean and reasonably priced. […]

I gave myself a cursory grooming and wandered back into town in search of dinner and diversion. I had an odd sense that I had been here before, which patently I had not. […] What made Weston feel familiar was, of course, that it was just like everywhere else. It had Boots and Marks & Spencer and Dixons and W.H. Smith and all the rest of it. I realized with a kind of dull ache that there wasn't a single thing here that I hadn't seen a million times already.

I went into a pub called the Britannia Inn, which was unfriendly without being actually hostile, and had a couple of lonely pints, then ate at a Chinese restaurant, not because I craved Chinese but because it was the only place I could find open. I was the only customer. As I quietly scattered rice and sweet and sour sauce across the tablecloth, there were some rumbles of thunder and, a moment later, the heavens opened – and I mean opened. I have seldom seen it rain so hard in England. […] Because I was a long walk from my hotel, I spun out the meal hoping the weather would ease off but it didn't, and eventually I had no choice but to step out into the rainy night.

[…] Pulling my jacket above my head, I waded out into the deluge, then sprinted across the street and impulsively took refuge in the first bright, open thing I came to – an amusement arcade. Wiping my glasses with a bandanna, I took my bearings. The arcade was a large room full of brightly pulsating machines, some of them playing electronic tunes or making unbidden *kerboom* noises, but apart from an overseer sitting at a counter with a drooping fag and a magazine, there was no-one in the place so it looked eerily as if the machines were playing themselves. […]

I had a strange hour in which I wandered in a kind of trance feeding money into machines and playing games I couldn't follow. […] Eventually I ran out of money and stepped out into the night.

'What impressions?' questions

You have learned that impressions are the views you might have of a place, person or organisation when you read what is being said about them. You have also learned that these impressions are created by the way details are given by the writer.

Now let us consider an exam question about impressions.

What impressions do you get of Weston-super-Mare from this passage? You must use the text to support your answer. [10]

To answer the question effectively, you need to look at the following points.

- **What the writer chooses to tell the reader about the town.** For example, Bryson visited the town on a rainy evening. Would the impression he gives have been different if he had arrived on a hot day at the weekend in the middle of summer? Remember, the writer has chosen which details to include so that he can create clear impressions for the reader.
- **How the article presents the details.** For example, Bryson mentions going into a pub and then into a Chinese restaurant, but he wants to give a particular impression of what they are like. How does he do this?

Activity 2

1   Copy and complete the table below. This will help to focus your reading of the passage.

What impressions do we get of the town?	What details from the passage give us this impression?
You are not likely to have a good time in the town if you visit	'the whole of Weston appeared to be indoors'
The hotels looked miserable	'didn't look particularly enticing'

2   Read the sample answer on page 44. The student sensibly begins by working through the passage from the beginning. However, the answer 'tracks the text' much less carefully after the opening three sentences and misses a lot of the detail.

3   Use what you have learned and the details and impressions you have collected in your table to write an answer to the following question about the passage on page 41.

What impressions do you get of Weston-super-Mare from this passage? You must use the text to support your answer. [10]

You should always try to look for a range of different impressions, each supported by at least one piece of evidence from the text.

Examiner tips

- Working carefully through the text helps you to select the evidence you need for your answer.
- You should then add your own comments, which strengthen your answer and will be rewarded by an examiner.
- It can be very helpful to begin an answer by using the words of the question. For example, 'The first impression I get of the town is...'.
- Remember that in an exam, even if you have lots of points to make, you must still complete the answer in about 12–13 minutes.

GradeStudio

Check your answer

- Did you find at least six impressions?
- Did you find some evidence to support the points you made?
- Did you look for the 'facts'?
- Did you also pick out some particular words and phrases?

Here is a student response to the exam task below. Read the answer and the examiner comments.

What impressions do you get of Weston-super-Mare from this passage? You must use the text to support your answer. [10]

Student 1

My first impression of Weston-super-mare is that it's one place you would want to avoid,✓ because it says 'the whole of Weston appeared to be indoors'✓, which suggests you would find it a miserable experience✓ to be there. It doesn't sound like a place people would want to go to, if it made you unhappy. Another impression you get from the passage is that it is like a ghost town.✓ There do not seem to be any people around and Bill Bryson states: 'The whole of Weston appeared to be indoors beyond drawn curtains.'✓ He says most of the hotels were 'dark and empty' so this also makes it sound like a ghost town.✓ He also says the ones that were open 'didn't look particularly enticing'.✓ In some places he makes it sound as though he does quite like the town because he says that it felt 'familiar' and it had all the kinds of shops that he likes to go in, like Boots and Marks and Spencer. He likes it because it's like the places he's seen a million times already, although he also has a 'dull ache' about it. He also says that the town doesn't have many amusement arcades because it was the first one he came to that he went in and 'fed money into machines and played games I couldn't follow'. He doesn't seem to like being in there.

Margin annotations:
- develops the point
- offers a clear impression
- quotation links to the impression well
- sensible comment from the text that uses evidence to support
- offers further evidence
- misreads this part of the text
- gets lost and confused
- just a weak stab at the text
- text not read closely enough

Examiner comments

This response begins well but shows a lack of close reading as it moves through the text. All the marks are gained in the first half of the answer, where the impressions are clearly stated and the student uses good supporting evidence from the passage. Notice that the word 'impression' from the question is only used in the first half of the answer. The last part of the answer shows some confusion and mis-reading, as the student thinks that Bill Bryson likes the fact that the town looks like any other town, which is incorrect, and struggles with the 'dull ache' that Bryson feels. Overall, this is a disappointing response, although it began very well.

'What impressions?' questions: how to improve your response

- To improve your response (as you may have seen from your own answer to this question), you need to try to identify a range of different impressions that are in the passage.
- You also benefit if you can use the text to support or prove your impressions are correct.
- It is important to read the text carefully so that you don't make the kinds of errors seen at the end of the answer opposite.
- Beginning some sentences with 'One impression that is given is...' can help you keep focused on the question.
- There will always be at least five or six separate points to make so it is important to work your way through in sequence.
- The answer shows some idea of what to do, particularly at first but it picks up few marks in the second half of the answer.

Putting it into practice

On your own or with a partner explain what you now know about:

- finding impressions in a text
- supporting your impressions by reference to the facts given in the text
- supporting your impressions by selecting and analysing key words and phrases

In the future:

- you must practise this type of question using a range of texts
- always start with an 'impression' (how you see something or someone)
- use details or facts from the article along with words/phrases to support your answer
- make sure you include at least five or six impressions
- aim to produce a complete answer in 12–13 minutes.

Your learning

This lesson will help you to:

- practise 'impressions' questions
- develop a secure technique for answering these questions.

When answering **'What impression?'** questions, remember you should always try to look for a range of different impressions and support each of them with facts and words/phrases from the text.

Activity 1

Read the extract alongside and then answer the question below.

What different impressions of Chris Moyles do you get from the newspaper interview? [10]

PROFILE **CHRIS MOYLES**

Chris Moyles interview: radio's best kept secret?

Examiner tips

- Do not waste words or time. Every sentence should be making a point that will gain a tick.
- Follow the passage in a logical sequence. Track the text line by line, using the information or details to link to the impressions you get of Chris Moyles from what is said.
- Use your own words where you can but include plenty of evidence from the passage.
- Check that you are linking your impressions to evidence from the passage.

Off air Chris Moyles, the headline-grabbing, over-paid Radio 1 DJ you love to hate, is reserved, likeable and – he says – worth every penny

Though the London sky is sagging with rain, Chris Moyles is sitting outside at a pavement table. He has just finished his breakfast show on Radio 1. [...] With his baseball cap pulled down and the collar of his adidas top zipped up, he looks more like a bouncer than one of the highest paid presenters at the BBC, but I suspect he tucks his neck in like this more out of self consciousness than an urge to present himself as a hard man. [...]

Moyles entertains some 7.7 million listeners every morning between 6.30 and 10. In terms of ratings, Sir Terry Wogan over on Radio 2 is still The Daddy. But the gap appears to be narrowing.

This comes as a surprise to anyone – which is pretty much everyone – who dismissed Moyles as an uncouth, Northern yob when he took over the Breakfast Show in 2004. [...]

Not only did he not lose listeners, he started to pile them on, billing himself modestly as the saviour of Radio 1.

'The saviour line was a gimmick,' he says. 'I don't want to be like the Spice Girls where they genuinely started discussing girl power.' This September he will have been doing the show for five years, beating Tony Blackburn's record.

And it is telling that when the BBC recently announced that its stars would be taking pay cuts, Moyles wasn't among them. [...]

Moyles is twitchy about the press, which is why he rarely gives interviews. 'There are people who profess to hate me who have never heard the show,' he says at one point. 'I find this hilarious and frustrating at the same time. What can I do?'

Activity 2

Read the following extract and then answer the question below.

What impressions does Tony Barrett give of what it is like for students preparing for their GCSE exams? [10]

Assess your progress with the peer/self-assessment activity opposite.

A GCSE in frustration

With weeks to go, exam season is getting too much for Tony Barrett

The libraries have never been so full of anxious faces, the cinemas and parks so devoid of bored teenagers. Students everywhere are stressed to the point they may explode at any given time while households are fraught with worried parents (not that they have anything to worry about). Meanwhile, siblings are getting together to laugh at their brothers and sisters as they try to remember what Stalin's policy of collectivisation was. Yes, it's that special time of the year again: exams.

Not that I need reminding, but I am at the start of my GCSEs and, through a combination of school and parents, I am being convinced that not doing well will put me on a slippery slope which will end on the streets or in prison (although the latter may be an improvement on spending four hours in the exam hall every day).

Home, as I fondly called it a couple of months ago, seems now like a red-brick prison; I stare out of my window at the 'normal' people walking past, or gaze absent-mindedly at the same bird for 20 minutes (my concentration span isn't the greatest), trying to remember what the properties of alkali metals and noble gases are (I still can't).

Try to go out the front door and you will be bombarded with a stream of questions so thick it's like an interrogation: 'Are you done revising?' 'Have you finished it all properly?' 'What about that business studies coursework?'

And, of course, the classic, rhetorical: 'Are you sure 20 minutes is really enough time to do your essay properly?' If you say yes, don't expect to be outside for a very long time. And when your little sister is laughing and pointing at you behind your parents' back, don't rise to it; then you're just taking your frustration out on your poor little sister, obviously. She hasn't done anything wrong, of course.

Everytime I try to go on MSN or MySpace, my copy of To Kill a Mockingbird winks at me, reminding me that I can't remember that all-important quote on page 100 (something about tolerance). That's the difference between a B and a C.

Unsurprisingly, school is no better. Every 20 minutes I'm told with authority: 'This will come up in the exam.' Really? Even better, it seems that doing this year's exam isn't enough. We have to do last year's for practice. And the year before that. And the year before that. And so on.

- Remember to work through the text line by line; some of the details may be grouped together in one sentence.
- The key to this question is the link between what you say about students and the evidence you use.
- Make sure that your answer is as clear and precise as you can make it.

A couple of years back, a speaker told us in an assembly: 'These are the most carefree years of your life.'

The emphasis has now shifted to: 'You have to do well this summer or you'll struggle to get a decent job – ever.' Looking at the mountain of books on my bedroom floor, all filled with barely-legible notes, you would have thought exams were life-or-death, or that the world would end if I can't get a B in maths. There is a noose tightened and at the ready if I dare get below a C in science.

Time slows down when you're doing exams. In the exam hall, you can do a five-page essay in a minute and spend the next two hours twiddling your thumbs, wondering what you've mucked up. Alternatively, you might be struggling during the exam and time, just for a laugh, rushes by, leaving you two minutes to write a page-long answer to how a fluctuating exchange rate can affect businesses in Britain that trade abroad.

It has even invaded our social side, the last aspect of life previously untouched by school. People are locking themselves up on Saturdays to plough through the coursework due in on Monday (although, before you start, you spend the obligatory three hours reflecting on how much you have to do). Nothing is untouched by the cold hand of exams.

Peer/Self-assessment activity

1 Check your answers to Activity 2.
- Did you find at least six impressions?
- Did you work through the text in a sequence?
- Did you find details in the text to support your impressions?
- Did you find any examples of particular words and phrases used by the writer?

2 Now try to mark your answer to Activity 2 using the mark scheme below to help you.

Improve your learning

8–10 marks
▶ Selects a range of detail that links well with a range of impressions about how students are affected.
▶ Answers are thorough and detailed.

6–7 marks
▶ Spots a range of valid details with one or two impressions.
▶ Better answers will begin to link impressions with evidence.

5–6 marks
▶ Collects a few of the details about how students spend their time.
▶ Struggles to identify impressions with the details.

3 Where are your strengths? Where is your answer not so strong? Make a list of one or two things you need to improve and practise these skills.

Your learning

This lesson will help you to:

- understand how texts present a viewpoint or attitude
- develop an approach to an 'attitude' question.

Writers often do more than present facts and information.
For example, a writer may:

- give lots of information about a town they have visited
- let readers know their opinion about the town as well. If they tell readers there is nothing to do in the evenings and the restaurants are often empty, it should be obvious that they have a negative view of the town and they probably think it's not worth a visit.

One of the frequently used types of exam questions will ask you to explain what the writer's attitude is and how this is made clear to the reader.

A question of this type may include the words 'attitude' or 'viewpoint' in it, but you are more likely to be asked to explain the writer's 'thoughts and feelings'.

When you answer this kind of question remember the following points.

- Work through the text line by line so that you can see the way thoughts and feelings develop.
- It is very useful to start your answer with 'At first the author thinks...' or 'the author feels...'. Beginning sentences in this way will help you to focus on the question. Then try to add comments (or inferences), which will gain reward.
- Each thought or feeling you identify must be supported by evidence from the text, such as a short, relevant quotation.
- Use the third person ('they' or 'the author') in your answer. Avoid using the first person ('I think' or 'I feel') as this will take you away from the question.
- Get into the habit of checking that your work includes a range of comments supported with evidence from the text.

Read the following article and then use Activity 1 on page 52 to help you answer the question on page 53.

The article was written by a journalist called Andrew Purvis, who writes about the week his two children, Lawrence and Rosie, spent on a PGL holiday.

With its crude wooden dormitories, ablutions blocks, flagpole and assault course, Marchant's Hill wasn't unlike the barracks where [my father had] begun his National Service. The camp, with its huts of Canadian cedar (referred to in the brochure as 'chalets'), had housed children evacuated from London's East End during the Second World War. The buildings were dotted randomly in the 40 acres of woodland, to make them harder to spot from the air during bombing raids.

After a quick tour with a 'groupie' (group leader), slightly marred by a girl a few years older than my two weeping distraughtly as her parents left, the Big Moment came. Lawrence, nine, had found his friend Richard, and was already on to the next thing (communal orange juice and games). 'Bye, Dad,' he said, with not a trace of emotion. Rosie, nearly two years younger, looked at me mistrustfully. There was a slight wobble of the lip then she threw herself into my arms. Next moment, she was off, sprinting excitedly towards the meeting point where the rising babble of a hundred children's voices made me glad I was getting in the car and going home.

But it was a difficult moment. Entrusting your children to complete strangers for a week isn't run-of-the-mill stuff, even for an absent father […]. As the car crunched across the gravel and we turned into the road, they were out of sight but not out of mind.

What they did in the next seven days is a mystery, illuminated only by the journals they kept and odd conversations about events half-remembered.

Lawrence was enrolled on the Newsflash course – film-making, photography, magazine production and the use of a recording studio (to use the word music would be misleading). Half of each day was spent doing climbing, abseiling, archery and mountain biking. Rosie chose the multi-activity programme – with all the emphasis on outdoor sports and rowdy games at the centre's two activity zones […].

When we collected the children the next Saturday, they were boisterous, sunkissed and filthy. […] In the car, I couldn't understand why they were shouting. Then it dawned on me: if you live for a week with a hundred children, you forget what a normal voice sounds like.

Activity 1

Read the table below, which shows some of the material you might use to answer the question on the 'thoughts and feelings' the writer has about the holiday.
Is there anything to add to the table?

Thoughts and feelings?	Evidence
He is not impressed by the holiday site (He **thinks** the place is not very impressive).	He talks about 'crude wooden dormitories'. It looked like a 'barracks'.
He **feels** worried about leaving his children in case they are upset or get home-sick.	He notices the girl who is 'weeping' as her parents leave. At first Rosie looks as though she might get upset – 'a slight wobble of the lip'.
He **feels** reassured when his children seem happy to be left there.	Lawrence had quickly 'found his friend'. He was quickly occupied by 'orange juice and games'. Rosie sprints off 'excitedly' when she sees other children.
He **feels** pleased to escape the noise of all the children in the camp.	Hearing all the noise of the children made him 'glad I was getting in the car and going home'.
He **knows** he will spend the week thinking (and worrying) about them.	He thinks about leaving his children with 'complete strangers' and says it will not be easy.
He **realises** they had had plenty to do.	Their journals suggested they took part in lots of different activities.
When he collects them he **feels pleased** they have had a great time.	They are 'boisterous'. They were 'sunkissed and filthy'.

Activity 2

Now answer the question below.

What are the writer's thoughts and feelings about the PGL holiday his children went on? [10]

Examiner tips

- In the exam you must write your answer in continuous prose.
- It is absolutely vital to focus on the question and keep the idea of 'thoughts and feelings' in view. For example, if you were to write that Andrew Purvis calls the chalets 'crude wooden dormitories', it would not earn you any reward. However, if you say, 'When he sees where his children will sleep, he thinks the buildings are horrible because they look like "crude wooden dormitories"', you would earn reward because you have identified his feelings and then used some detail from the passage to support your view.
- You do not need to begin every sentence of your answer with 'He thinks' or 'He feels' but if you make sure you have those words in most sentences, you will almost certainly be answering the question.

GradeStudio

Here is a student response to the exam task below. Read the answer and the examiner comments.

What are the writer's thoughts and feelings about the PGL holiday his children went on? [10]

Extract typical of a C grade answer

Student 1

When he arrives at the camp, Andrew Purvis describes the place in a way that shows he thinks it's not a very nice place.✓ Firstly, he uses the word 'crude' to describe the dormitories✓. and later he said that many things on site made the centre look like a 'barracks'.✓ I know that army barracks are not very nice places to be and you wouldn't want a holiday in them.✓. He thinks that leaving his children at the camp is not easy. He must have felt worried✓ because he thought his daughter was going to cry,✓ even though his son had found a friend quickly. He would have felt pleased that his son joined in quickly✓ but Rosie was only seven and he might not have been sure she would like it on her own. His point of view about the centre changed when his children said how much they enjoyed learning new things.✓ Lawrence enrolled on the Newsflash course✓ and he thinks Rosie must have enjoyed what she did because of what she wrote in her journal.✓. He thinks they must have enjoyed themselves because they were 'boisterous'✓ in the car and 'shouting'✓ about their holiday, so he would feel glad✓ they had a good time.

Annotations:
- shows his thoughts about the place very clearly
- offers supporting evidence
- sensible overview comment
- further support from the text
- shows how he is feeling
- shows why he felt worried
- shows a different feeling here
- offers evidence why his feelings changed
- notes his change of feelings
- more evidence
- evidence to support his feelings

Examiner comments

This is a really thorough answer from the candidate.

Strong points
- This tracks the text really carefully; almost nothing is missed.
- Almost every sentence is earning marks.
- Where the writer's thoughts and feelings are given, they are usually supported with evidence; in some cases, additional evidence is offered.
- There is no waffle or waste in this answer. It does exactly what the question asks.

Viewpoint and attitude: how to improve your response

To improve your response always keep a clear focus on the question.

- Highlight key words in the question if you find it helpful. The key words here are 'writer's thoughts and feelings'.
- There will always be a range of 'thoughts and feelings' or 'attitudes' so check that you include different feelings or attitudes.
- Use the passage to prove that the 'thoughts and feelings' you have identified are correct.
- Try to get used to the pattern of 'comment + evidence' in your sentences.
- Do not give up after one or two thoughts or feelings. There will always be **at least** five or six separate points to make so work through the text line by line.
- The answer shows how to gain a really good mark by being methodical and matching evidence to a comment wherever you can.

Putting it into practice

On your own or with a partner explain what you now know about:

- finding the writer's 'attitudes' or 'thoughts and feelings' in a text
- supporting your ideas by reference to the text
- supporting your ideas by selecting and analysing key words and phrases.

In the future:

- you must practise this type of question using a range of texts
- always start with a 'thought' or 'feeling'
- use textual evidence to support your answer
- make sure you include a range of thoughts and feelings
- follow the text in sequence
- aim to produce a complete answer in 12–13 minutes.

Peer/Self-assessment activity

1 What thoughts and feelings and evidence has the student used in their answer?

2 Note down any points you missed which could have earned you a mark.

3 How could you improve next time?

Your learning

This lesson will help you to:

- practise 'attitude' questions
- develop a secure approach to 'attitude' questions.

When answering an 'attitude' question:

- you must keep your focus on the writer's 'attitudes' or 'thoughts and feelings'
- it is sensible to use 'they think' or 'they feel' as a way of staying in focus on the question
- use evidence to support what you say but remember that the details and quotations from the text are not enough on their own.

Activity 1

Read this extract and answer the question below.

What are the writer's thoughts and feelings about an Astley Woods holiday? [10]

Examiner tips

- You should spend no more than 12–13 minutes on this question.
- Make sure that your answer is focused on the question. Use 'they think' or 'they feel' (it really does work).
- The key to this question is to identify a range of thoughts and feelings.
- Follow what the writer is saying step by step, selecting relevant material.
- Each thought or feeling needs to be clearly linked to evidence in the text.
- Use the words of the question as your 'way in'.

Astley Woods – holiday review

The appeal of Astley Woods is that it is 'in the wild'. Actually, their sites are pretty much in the middle of nowhere, though this is sold as an attraction because you can 'get away from it all'. To be fair, the site we visited was set in glorious woodland with lots of nature trails and plenty of wildlife to try and spot.

There are number of choices in accommodation to suit your budget. At the bottom of the price range is the 'Wychwood Forest' chalet, up to the most expensive 'New Forest' chalets that have things like a DVD in the cabin, private parking, and their own hot tub. The chalets are not the most attractive wooden buildings, but ours was clean and homely, although I heard one visitor complain that her chalet had a fusty smell and had dirty marks on the walls and doors. On arrival one of the first things I recommend is getting down to the Woods Market, which is a reasonably priced, well-stocked shop that sells freshly baked goods and the range of food that you're likely to find in small supermarkets.

One of the problems with Astley Woods is that it can get quite expensive, depending on what you want to do. It's true that it can be a relatively cheap week if you're happy just going to the pool, walking round the site and eating in. However, if you want to try your hand at the kinds of activities that are on offer, they do not come cheap. For example, quad biking was £35 for an hour and massages were £30 for 30 minutes. Activities I would

recommend are the horse riding lessons and the archery, which I really enjoyed, but it's advisable to book activities in advance, because the popular ones get booked up very quickly.

There's lots to do and many of the activities are suitable for children or those with families. You can also hire bikes, and it was good to be able to cycle all around the site and on the nature trails, though I thought £22 each for a bike (Mon–Fri) was very expensive. Another problem was that the bikes all looked similar so do try to remember where you park – one day I spent half an hour looking round trying to find my bike.

One annoying thing for me about the two Astley Woods centres I visited was that they seemed to be constantly under construction. I imagine this is kept to a minimum in peak season but as a visitor going in the cheap season I found various problems such as roads in the centre closed off, and for two days the pool was shut down for maintenance.

The restaurants have varied menus and plenty of choices, but they are all quite expensive. One of the complaints I heard from visitors was that the restaurants often seemed to be under-staffed, and there were grumbles about slow service.

So is it worth it? Well, if you love swimming and hanging about a pool I suppose it is pretty good. Walking or cycling round the park is enjoyable except for all the noisy people which doesn't quite match the tranquil image presented in the Astley Woods brochure. Overall, it is probably worth going to one of the centres for a few days away if you have never been before, and it's good if you have children and are willing to pay – quite a lot – for some of the extra things on offer. Having done it once though, I'm not sure I'd go back.

Peer/Self-assessment activity

I Check your answers to Activity I.
- Did you find a range of thoughts and feelings?
- Did you work through the text in a sequence?
- Did you find evidence to support each of your comments?
- Did you find any examples of particular words and phrases used by the writer?

2 Now try to mark your answer to Activity I using the mark scheme below to help you.

⊙ Improve your learning

8–10 marks
▸ Selects details from the text to show understanding of the writer's thoughts and feelings.
▸ Better answers show a good range of evidence and stay focused on the question.

5–6 marks
▸ Makes simple comments based on surface features of text.
▸ Shows awareness of the writer's different thoughts and feelings.
▸ Some focus on the question.

2–3 marks
▸ Very short, brief answers.
▸ Selects a few details but may not link to thoughts and feelings.

Your learning

This lesson will help you to:

- understand the methods writers use to persuade readers
- learn how to approach this type of question.

Persuasive writers use many methods to encourage their readers to see their viewpoints. The exam questions often ask you to analyse how a text does this. It could be selling a product, trying to win your support or promoting an idea.

As you read a text, think what the text is about but focus on how the writer is trying to persuade, interest or influence you. You need to show the examiner that you can see how they are trying to do these things.

The questions are likely to be worded as follows.

- How does this text try to **persuade** or **attract** or **sell** or **influence**?
- How does the writer try to **encourage** or **interest** or **argue**?

There are four main areas to think about when you look at persuasive texts:

1 content (what the text is about)
2 language and tone (the choice of words and the way they are used)
3 headlines and titles
4 pictures and presentation.

Activity 1

1 Learn the four areas listed above as this will help you in the exam.
2 Read the extract opposite with the boxed comments. The extract is part of a leaflet advertising the Jorvik Viking Centre in York.

   Now answer the exam question below:

   How does this leaflet try to persuade the reader to visit the Jorvik Viking Centre? [10]

   Use the boxed comments to help you write your answer. Try to include additional comments of your own and support them with details from the text.

Examiner tips

- The best way to go about answering this type of question is to 'track' the text. Take each paragraph or section in turn. Think about **what** the text is telling you, **why** it might persuade or influence you, and **how** that is being done.
- Everything in a text like this is included for a reason. Your job is to look closely at everything.
- The question is asking you to consider how a writer tries to persuade. It is *not* asking whether you agree or not. You must look at what the writer is doing. Do not give your own views on the issue.
- Make sure you particularly focus on content and language/tone in your answer. There will usually be something to say about any headlines and the pictures but don't spend all of your time on these.

EXPERIENCE THE REAL THING

At JORVIK Viking Centre you are standing on the site of an astounding archaeological discovery. Thirty years ago our archaeologists revealed the houses, workshops and backyards of the Viking Age city of Jorvik. They couldn't believe their eyes!

Our experts excavated eight tonnes of deposits and unearthed 40,000 Viking objects, preserved in remarkably good condition. Then they studied these in such detail that we can now bring you as close as possible to a real experience of Viking life.

TRAVEL BACK 1000 YEARS...

on board your time machine and journey through the backyards and houses leading to the bustling streets of Jorvik. Everything here is based on facts – from the working craftsmen, the language of the gossiping neighbours, the smells of cooking and the cesspit!

Travel through the busy marketplace, experience a blast of smoke as you pass the blacksmith's furnace. Smell the fish on the riverside and visit the hearth scene inside the Viking home.

GET INVOLVED

Are you a Viking? NEW EXHIBITION
Work out if you have Viking ancestors using scientific and archaeological evidence. Visit the Viking Age riverside, the centre of immigration, trade and travel, and talk with our resident merchants.

Artefacts Alive:
Hosted by our holographic Viking ghosts, here you view 800 Viking-Age finds and work out how they were used in everyday Viking-Age life. Delve deeper with our six interactive IT installations.

Unearthed:
Discover the secrets of bones. Picture Viking-Age life, death, battle and disease through the examination of 10–11th century bones. Talks with the archaeologists throughout the day.

The heading suggests you will feel as though you are taking part in history; 'real' emphasises that what you see and touch in the Viking Centre will be authentic in every detail.

This image suggests you will see everything exactly as it would have been.

The word 'astounding' suggests what is there is exceptional and visitors will be amazed.

This content persuades visitors that they are on a real archaeological site; the dig happened where the visitors will be standing.

The sounds, smells and sights described here persuade the visitor that they will experience the details of everyday life as a Viking.

The heading indicates that visitors can take an active part in the exhibition.

The word 'ancestors' suggests that the experience can be made personal and so even more interesting.

The tone aims to persuade the reader that the visit will be an exciting experience.

Persuasive content

Content is a very important feature of any text. Almost all questions will focus on content to some extent.

The content of a persuasive text could include the following features:

- facts and opinions (what is said, how the material has been chosen, the points writers select to illustrate what they mean)
- the use of examples
- the use of statistics or figures
- the arguments used by the writer
- the use of quotations (often experts or personalities such as Lewis Hamilton or Jamie Oliver to give 'celebrity endorsement' and encourage others to follow their example)
- the problem and the solution – and how you can be part of the solution.

When you look at a text that is trying to persuade, identify the features above. Ask the following questions.

- Why is each feature used?
- What effect does each feature have? How does it persuade?

In your answer, mention the features or techniques. Always back them up with specific examples from the text. Always explain what effect they have.

Activity 1

Read the text on page 62. It is trying to persuade the reader that it is acceptable for animals to be in circuses. Look at the question below.

How does Dea Birkett try to persuade you to support circuses? [10]

To tackle this question, you need to:

- read the text carefully
- select relevant material that will go in your answer
- consider how your selected details are intended to persuade the reader.

Use the table below to help you. It shows examples of details from the text that are used to persuade the reader and how they do this. You may be able to add extra details or comments about how the details persuade.

Details from the text	How the details persuade
The writer uses facts and opinions	
'the park... was transformed into a world of wondrous, exotic people and beasts'.	The writer suggests circuses created an exotic, fantastic world.
'there was no magical kingdom springing up overnight in our park'.	The writer links circuses with the magic of childhood.
	She suggests that the disappearance of the circus means that something magical has been lost, especially for children.
The writer uses statistics	
'There are now fewer than half-a-dozen circuses with animals left in Britain'.	The writer tells us a fact about the decline in circuses.
The writer uses opinions	
'Animal-rights groups have waged a war against circus in Britain'.	The writer tells us that we have been tricked by animal-rights groups that have campaigned against circuses.
The writer uses examples	
'On most opening nights, protestors distribute RSPCA leaflets outside the circus gates'.	The writer gives an example that she thinks shows how the animal-rights groups behave.

Now write up your answer. Make sure you link the details from the text to how they persuade. Remember that in the exam you would only have about 12–13 minutes to write your answer. You need to work quickly as well as carefully.

> **Examiner tips**
>
> - Do not always repeat 'the writer says...' to state what the writer is doing.
> - Use some of the following verbs. They can be a more exact way to introduce how the writer is trying to win over the reader:
>
> | | | |
> |---|---|---|
> | describes | suggests | compares |
> | mentions | shows | gives (details/examples) |
> | tells | insists | emphasises |
>
> uses (examples/facts/statistics/quotations/irony/humour/personal experience).

The show must go on

Once upon a time, a little girl saw the circus parade pass the end of her street. Within hours, the park where she played was transformed into a world of wondrous, exotic people and beasts. She saw men walking on stilts and wobbling on a high wire, clowns squelching, white horses teetering on their hind legs and an elephant strolling round a sawdust ring. […]

I was that little girl, and as I grew older fewer and fewer elephants paraded past the end of my road. Soon, there was no magical kingdom springing up overnight in our park. The rhythm of suburban life was no longer interrupted by fantastical eruptions. The circus had left our town forever.

There are now fewer than half-a-dozen circuses with animals left in Britain. In less than 20 years, an extraordinary two-century-old art form has been near-obliterated. Animal-rights groups have waged a war against circus in Britain, and circus people have been indiscriminately denounced as animal abusers. The opponents of circus have clearly won the propaganda war. Now, the most common image of the circus is not the magic, but the misery. Instead of fabulous feats by human and animal, we imagine elephants chained to pallets, incarcerated big cats and horses trapped in tiny stalls. […]

Pet owners may train their dogs to do tricks, but a Labrador scampering round a sawdust ring is considered an outrage. […]

On most opening nights, protestors distribute RSPCA leaflets outside the circus gates, and the local RSPCA office displays posters, 'DON'T GO TO THE CIRCUS'. […]

Martin Lacey [the owner of Circus Harlequin] recognises the picture in the RSPCA leaflet as his tigers, even though they don't name him and have never brought a complaint against Circus Harlequin. […]

Other forms of animal husbandry remain free from such censure. The RSPCA's response to last year's Grand National, when four horses died as a result of the race, was to talk to and advise the Jockey Club. The RSPCA has no policy to outlaw horse racing: instead, it negotiates for better conditions with those responsible for the horses' welfare. Its position in circuses, however, is non-negotiable.

'It's ludicrous. They're hypocrites,' says Tommy Pinder, in uncharacteristically strong language. 'If I took my horses and – God forbid – just one died in the ring, there'd be an outcry. I'd probably be sent to prison. But because a big event like the Grand National […] is sponsored by the upper class and royalty and all that, nothing's said about it. But we're easy targets, we're very easy targets for the RSPCA.' […]

Outside Britain, the show goes on. In France, Switzerland, Germany, Italy, Spain and all over Scandinavia, circus flourishes. […]

The circus people I met were not elephant-beating barbarians. They were a small, disenfranchised people, struggling to survive against odds that would have defeated almost anyone else. […] Instead of shouting outside the circus gates, instead of leaning on councils, animal-rights groups should sit down and talk.

Once upon a time, at the end of my road, there was a parade of elephants. Today I imagine holding my daughter's hand, as we stand outside our home staring up at these fabulous beasts. It happens all over Europe. It can happen here.

Here are two student responses to the exam task below. Read the answers and the examiner comments.

How does Dea Birkett try to persuade you to support circuses? [10]

Student 1

weak start: not answering the question set

sensible comment

Dea Birkett's way of persuading you to support circuses is good. ✗ She uses her childhood memories as examples of how good the circus really is. ✓ She talks about remembering the circus going past the end of her street and the park being full of horses, elephants and men on stilts. ✓ She wants us to support circuses because she calls them 'an extraordinary two-centry-old art form', showing she thinks they should be kept. ✓ She is sorry that there are less than half-a-dozen circuses left in Britain today because of animal rights protesters and the RSPCA. ✓ She says that every time there is a circus in town, the RSPCA give out leaflets and 'Don't go to the circus' are displayed. ✓
Tommy Pinder says, 'They're hypocrites' because although four horses died in the Grand National, he knows that 'if just one of my horses died in the ring, there'd be an outcry.' ✓ Dea Birkett goes on to tell about the circuses in France, Switzerland and Germany. ✓

evidence to support comment

selects a detail but no real comment

needs to link to 'how'

selects detail but not linked to a comment about 'how'

another detail

Examiner comments

The answer makes use of the passage but struggles to link the details with comments about how they would persuade the reader. The answer tends to tell us what Dea Birkett said rather than how she persuades us. There is some reward for selecting some relevant details but because it doesn't really explore **how** the writer tries to persuade.

Peer/Self-assessment activity

1 Which response is your answer closest to?

2 How could you improve next time?

Student 1

suggests the magic of the circus

gives her view of the problem

explores the impact of language used

sees why the comparison is made, but could link to 'how'

understands why the quotation supports her case

spots the detail and sees how they are stereotyped

Dea Birkett tries to persuade us to persuade circuses by telling us of her early memories about the circus by saying her park was transformed into 'a world of wondrous, exotic people and beasts.' ✓ She's saying it was out of this world, totally different, like something you can only imagine. ✓ She mentions the elephants 'strolling around', saying they look casual and nothing is wrong with them. ✓ The writer also leaves a paragraph at the end about her memory of holding her daughter's hand and watching the 'fabulous beasts'. ✗ Dea says circuses today are fading away because animal rights groups have tricked people into believing animals are treated cruelly. ✓ She states 'tricked' like they are lying about the circus. ✓ She compares house trained dogs who know tricks to circus dogs performing tricks, how it's an outrage. ✓ Dea makes us feel sorry for the people who pitch their caravans and are persecuted by protesters and with violence, trying to make the protesters look like the bad guys. ✓ Dea compares the circus to the Grand National, saying that more horses die in the racing than at the circus and says that the RSPCA have no policy to stop that. ✓ She also tries to persuade us by interviewing circus owner, Tommy Pinder. He states that the only reason the RSPCA are after them is because they're easy targets, the horse racing is sponsored by royalty, saying they're hypocrites and making them look bad. ✓ Dea states that other countries have huge businesses in circuses and it is very important to them ✓ and she also states the people she has met so far 'aren't elephant-beating barbarians'. ✓ They're 'struggling to exist', saying from experience they are not bad people, they are just trying to feed their families. ✓

develops the point further

focuses on specific words to suggest they were not treated cruelly

this is not developed enough

uses the example to support her viewpoint

understands 'how' but might have pushed on to give examples

spots the detail but could have pushed on to explain why this would persuade

sees how Birkett is trying to gain sympathy for them

Examiner comments

This is an excellent response that has good, methodical coverage of the text, with some very clear explorations of how Dea Birkett has tried to persuade the reader. The comments are made clearly and they are well supported by the 'evidence' from the text itself. There are some telling examples where the impact of particular words or phrases are explored, and although in one or two places the details are 'spotted' rather than explored, it is hard to see what more could have been done in the 12–13 minutes the student had to write this.

Language used to influence

The choice of content is part of how a writer persuades a reader but the language that is used and the way in which it is used are just as important. For example, a word such as 'tricked' can be very powerful in affecting how you think about a subject. When you look at the language of persuasive texts, you need to look for key words and phrases, but you also need to think about their purpose and effect.

Activity 1

Read the short extracts opposite. They are taken from web pages advertising the resorts.

1　Make a list of the facts, statistics or figures that are included in each of the texts.

2　How else do you think the texts are trying to make the resorts sound attractive?

You will probably see from these examples that while some facts and figures may be used, it is the way the information is presented that begins to persuade the reader. The choice of particular words and phrases in these texts becomes really important in trying to persuade the reader to want to visit.

Activity 2

1　Look again at the three short texts. Make a list of words or phrases that you feel are being used to suggest how good the resort is. Then try to decide what is the intended effect of each word or phrase.

For example, when the Blackpool text tells readers the town is 'bursting with thrills, excitement and entertainment', it is suggesting that visitors would find so many exciting things to do that they will never be bored.

Collecting the details in two columns will help you, so organise your notes in a table like the one below.

Words or phrases used	The intended effect (how it persuades)
'bursting with thrills, excitement and entertainment'.	You will never be short of things to do.

Blackpool – Feel the Buzz

BLACKPOOL is buzzing – Britain's family holiday capital is bursting with thrills, excitement and entertainment.

The nation's most popular beach resort – which attracts more than 10 million visitors a year – is forging ahead with a growing diary of fabulous world-class events to enhance its fantastic attractions, top entertainment and sensational live shows.

These are exciting times as visitors take a fresh look at Blackpool – famous for its Tower and Promenade, seven miles of award-winning beaches, the magic of the Illuminations and its warm and friendly welcome.

Welcome *to Greater Yarmouth*

Welcome to Greater Yarmouth, where 15 miles of golden sandy beaches stretch out into the horizon along an ever changing coastline, from seaside amusements to rugged cliffs, from the serenity of Scroby Sands windfarm and seal colony, to the fast paced action of Marine Parade. [...]

10 Come and enjoy sandy beaches, fun outdoor and inside attractions from theme parks to crazy golf, from gardens to museums, a fabulous choice of places to eat and drink, a bustling town centre and charming quayside, all within easy walking distance.

Just a few miles from the resort centre pretty Norfolk villages and the beautiful winding Norfolk Broads waterways, lined with traditional 15 windmills of all shapes and sizes, are just waiting to be explored.

Welcome to Southend-on-Sea

With seven glorious miles of seafront, the longest pleasure pier in the world and a host of exciting events and festivals all year, it's no wonder Southend-on-Sea leaves visitors smiling time after time.

Here you'll find all the traditional seaside pleasures as well as exhilarating watersports, theme park thrills, top shopping, thriving arts and culture, dazzling night-life and a feast of seafood. Choose from more than 300 great places to eat, and quality accommodation from luxury hotels to guest houses and bed & breakfast.

Activity 3

Work with a partner. Take it in turns to work through the text opposite. Find the words or phrases you think are trying to persuade readers to visit. The text is taken from a website advertising the resort.

Words or phrases used	The intended effect (how it persuades)

You should by now be an expert in spotting the kinds of words and phrases that writers use to attract visitors or to sell their products. More importantly, you are becoming aware of **how** these words or phrases persuade. In the next activity, you are going to show how effective you can be at this type of persuasive writing.

Activity 4

Imagine you have the job of persuading visitors to visit your seaside resort, Astley-by-Sea. You have to write the first 200 words on the Astley-by-Sea website. You can use words and phrases from any of the texts on pages 67 and 69 and invent any details you think will attract huge numbers of visitors to Astley-by-Sea.

Remember, you have a maximum of 200 words, so, just like the texts you have read, everything you write must convince the reader it's a great place to visit!

visitilfracombe.co.uk

Ilfracombe North Devon's Premier Resort

Ilfracombe is the perfect location for North Devon holidays, offering you a gateway to an exciting blend of stunning coastal scenery, seaside fun, rural tranquility and centuries of heritage and style. There is a tremendous choice of accommodation, from luxury hotels to quality guest houses and bed and breakfasts to self catering cottages, holiday parks and caravan and camping sites.

Ilfracombe is the 'jewel' of the North Devon coast and a remarkable location for romantic getaways, family holidays or activity breaks.

A Coast of Contrasts

Ilfracombe is a stunning coastal town with white washed houses, grand Victorian villas and terraces. Nestling between the National Park of Exmoor to the East and the golden coast with the surfing beaches to the West.

A place where you can come and relax, where the sky meets the Atlantic Ocean. A resort that also has a contemporary edge from its top class restaurants and galleries, to its theatre and night life. Ilfracombe is a place to experience and be seen.

Wake up to Ilfracombe – a great location, offering you superb Devon hospitality and quality accommodation. Once you have visited our town, Ilfracombe will be your choice for North Devon holidays for years to come.

Peer/Self-assessment activity

1 Check your answers to Activity 4.
  - Did you manage to use a range of words that made the resort sound impressive?
  - Did you try to balance the range of content with the persuasive language you employed?

2 Work with a partner and compare the persuasive language you used in each of your answers. Are there words that seem to be used frequently? Why is this? Look at the range of points you included in the content and discuss whether there are ways of making the result even more attractive to the reader.

Persuasive headlines and titles

Your learning

This lesson will help you to:

- understand how headlines and titles influence readers
- link comments to headlines and titles.

In addition to commenting on the content and language of a text, you may comment on the headline or titles. You will find these most often in a newspaper article or a leaflet.

- Most headlines and titles are in big, bold writing. They will try to catch the reader's attention by saying something short and snappy. You will get no reward if you simply tell the marker these things.
- Instead, explain **how** the headline or title makes its impact or captures interest. It is worth asking yourself: what does it say; what's unusual about the way it says it; why is that interesting or how does it catch the reader's attention?

Headlines are often used to introduce a topic clearly, but they may also try to persuade, amuse or shock you. Common features of headlines and titles are the following, some of which can be seen in the examples in Activity I.

- They speak directly to the audience (using 'you' to engage the reader as an individual).
- They are often in the form of questions (sometimes rhetorical but often direct).
- They use sensational or dramatic language or words with emotional content to catch the reader's eye.
- They may play on words, often in a witty way (using puns, alliteration, rhyme and so on).

Activity 1

Below are some real headlines. Explain what you think each of the articles was about and why the headlines are effective.

(a) **Let's get Fizzical**

(b) **Just 16 actors per episode as EastSpenders is forced to cut back**

(c) **'Even monkeys' can get A-levels**

Examiner tips

- Do not worry if you cannot think of anything useful to say about a particular headline. It is more important to focus on the content and the language of the article.
- If you do comment on it, say **why** or **how** it impacts on the reader. You will get no marks for just saying a headline is 'big and bold and makes you want to read on'.
- The effect of a headline can be better described using words such as 'provocative', 'arresting', 'challenging', 'intriguing', 'tasteless', 'funny' or 'sensational'.

Here is an example of a headline and the sub-heading that went with it. It came from a newspaper report.

Going the Distance

At this year's London marathon, Fauja Singh aims to beat his best time of six hours. It seems a modest ambition – but then, he is 93. Anne Johnson finds out what drives him.

Here are two examples of what students said about the headline above.

Student 1

The writer tries to make this an interesting article by using a big, bold, catchy headline, 'Going the distance'. This is catchy because when a person sees this headline they will like to see what it is about. The sub-heading also make the reader want to know more because this creates a 'wow' inside the reader and they want to read more about this 93 year old man.

Examiner comments

The problem here is that the comments are very vague. There is no attempt to say anything specific about the headline or what it might suggest. It is hard to imagine any headline that is not 'big and bold', and the comment about it being 'catchy' is again too vague. The comment on the sub-heading would earn some reward for hinting at the surprise readers would feel about the marathon being run by a 93-year-old, but there is not very much to reward here.

Student 2

The headline 'Going the distance' suggests that the article has something to do with long distances and it also suggests completing something that's been started, but because it is not clear what it's about you would want to read the sub-heading. This is like a small summary and we are surprised at first because it sounds as if the article is about someone who runs very slowly, but then we are told this runner is 93, and she emphasises this by using a dash '– but then, he is 93', which would make us curious to know about such an old man running such a long distance.

Examiner comment

This is much better and it is clearly trying to look at the words of the headline and what they might suggest, and at how sub-heading would attract the reader. This student is aware that some of the information is not immediately revealed to the reader, and the key piece of information, the man's age, is not revealed until the end of the second sentence in the sub-heading. A marker would be impressed by the careful probing of headline and sub-heading and this would get the student off to a very good start in their answer.

Persuasive pictures and layout

Photographs and drawings send messages to the reader. The messages may be obvious or not easy to see. In a persuasive text illustrations are always there for a reason: to help strengthen a message or to link to the content and language.

A picture may be intended to shock, to attract or to stimulate an emotion in the reader. It is not enough just to note the existence of a picture, or simply to say what is in the picture. Always try to work out the **intention** and the **effect** of pictures in texts. Some articles have more than one picture, and you should consider all of them in your response.

When looking at pictures, ask yourself the following questions.

1 Why this picture? What is its effect?
2 Is each picture giving the same message?
3 How do the pictures work together to strengthen the message of the text?
4 Do the pictures give different messages? If so, why?

Remember, a picture will usually link to the headline and the main text.

Activity 1

Have a look at the pictures alongside and opposite and answer the questions below.

1 Why do you think each picture might have been chosen? What is its effect?

2 Does the picture with a headline strengthen the message of the headline? If so, why/how?

3 Think of headlines to go with the other three pictures.

Give water. Give life. Give £2 a month.

Presentation

Presentation

Presentation is not usually the most important of the ways in which a writer makes a text persuasive. Occasionally there is something useful to say, but do not get sidetracked. Look for:

- layout of text (bullets, fonts, text boxes)
- logos
- use of bold type or colour.

Always ask: 'What is the point or the effect of this?'

One of these features may be used to draw attention to a particular point. For example, the purpose of a logo is to help the reader recognise the brand and so feel confident in the content that it supports.

Activity 1

Work in pairs. For each logo opposite, answer the following questions.

1 Why do you think the organisation chose this logo?

2 What does the logo suggest to you?

3 Do you think it is an effective logo? Why? Why not?

Comments on presentation should only be a small part of your overall answer. The appearance and presentation of a text may attract your attention or catch your interest, but that is only the first part of the job. The really important part is how the presentation supports the content, language and pictures in **persuading** the reader. Nobody is likely to be persuaded by a text simply because of its layout.

Putting together the persuasive techniques

Now it is time to put together all that you have learnt about persuading readers.

Activity 1

Read the leaflet opposite carefully, then answer the question below.

How does the leaflet try to persuade you to visit Warwick Castle? [10]

You should consider:

- what the leaflet says you can see and do
- the choice of words used to persuade you
- the use of illustrations/pictures.

1. Work in pairs. Write down the main points you think your answer to the exam question should include.

2. Then, on your own, in a maximum of 12–13 minutes, write an answer to the question.

Examiner tips

The question itself will usually remind you to explore the key areas: content, language, pictures and presentation, so when you come to write your answer, it is sensible to write it in that order. When you are practising for the exam, you may find it helpful to make notes with those areas as headings.

IMAGINE A TOTALLY ELECTRIFYING, FULL DAY OUT AT BRITAIN'S ULTIMATE CASTLE.

Where you can immerse yourself in a thousand years of jaw-dropping history – come rain or shine.

Where ancient myths and spell-binding tales will set your imagination alight and your hair on end. Where princesses are pampered and maidens are wooed.

Experience the heat of battle at such close quarters you'll almost smell the fear, as winners become true heroes and losers are confined to dark, dank dungeons to be forgotten for eternity.

It could only be Warwick Castle.

KINGMAKER

How would you feel if you were preparing for what might be your last day on earth? Richard Neville, Kingmaker and Earl of Warwick, is thinking just that as he prepares his extensive household for the Battle of Barnet in 1471. Walk through the household and meet Fortune, Neville's mighty warhorse. See the Armourers at work, making chain mail, and the ladies of the wash house as they sing while they work. As the Kingmaker rallies his troops will you decide to join him in battle or run whilst you can…?

THE GAOL

When you descend into the airless, dark, damp dungeon in the depths of the Castle you leave the outside world behind. Down in the dungeon you can't hear anything – and no-one outside can hear you… Be thankful you can walk out again as many who made the journey before you didn't. If you have the stomach for it, a walk through the Torture Chamber will tell you all you need to know about medieval torture, if you want to know!

MILL AND ENGINE HOUSE

Originally built in the 12th century, the Mill and Engine House brought electric light to the Castle for the first time in 1894. Now the Mill is restored to its former glory. Meet the Mill Manager and discover for yourself how electricity was generated to light up the Castle.

THE PRINCESS TOWER

Magic and delight can be found around every corner of our new attraction, home to our very own fairytale princess, Princess Arabella. The Princess Tower is the perfect place for all little princesses.

ROYAL WEEKEND PARTY

Journey through a meticulous recreation of a Victorian house party and see some of the most respected and revered figures of society in the late 1800s. Guests and household staff alike are preparing for a lavish party, although for some dinner and drinks are not the only things on their mind – find out for yourself some of the intrigue, gossip and scandal surrounding the guests.

THE GREAT HALL AND STATE ROOMS

The cavernous Great Hall and six lavishly decorated State Rooms sit at the very heart of the Castle, bringing to life the history of the Castle's treasures and those who have called the Castle their home.

GROUNDS AND GARDENS

The Castle's grounds and gardens provide a tranquil setting at any time of the year. The Castle has 60 acres for visitors to enjoy – from the 'Capability' Brown landscape of the Pageant Field with the Conservatory and the Peacock Garden, to the River Island where a menagerie was once housed.

TOWERS AND RAMPARTS

Scale the towers and ramparts and enjoy stunning views of the Castle and the town of Warwick. Here you can really imagine yourself as a medieval bowman ready to defend the Castle – waiting on the ramparts with your bow, for the enemy to approach and for you to take aim.

GradeStudio

Here is a student response to the exam task below. Read the answer and the examiner comments.
How does the leaflet try to persuade you to visit Warwick Castle? [10]

Extract typical of a C grade answer

Student 1

The leaflet tries to persuade people to visit Warwick Castle by first of all having a heading that makes a day at the castle sound fantastic. The word 'ultimate' suggests you won't find another place like it ✓ and it makes it sound as though you will be in the middle of real-life castle action: 'Experience the heat of battle at such close quarters you'll almost smell the fear...' ✓

selects and comments on specific choice of language

supports a comment with detail from the text

The attraction, Kingmaker, would persuade more of a younger reader to want to go there because they would possibly be interested in the way people prepared for a battle in those times ✓ and in the last line of that paragraph it says, 'Will you decide to join him in battle or run whilst you can?' This would make someone feel part of the event, ✓ although it is false.

again, specific selection and who/why it would attract

The GAOL would attract men and boys because it sounds scary and almost like a challenge daring you to go there, ✓ 'If you have the stomach for it...' ✓ so boys would want to think they are tough enough to go into such a horrible place. ✓ Although castles would mainly attract boys, the 'Princess Tower' would persuade girls to visit. All girls would like to be a princess, and if they visit they will get a chance to see 'Princess Arabella', ✓ which sounds like something from a child's fairy story.

probing 'how' the texts engages the potential visitor

explains why it would persuade

builds and develops the comment

The 'Royal Weekend Party' would attract people who wanted to see how rich people held parties in Victorian times and see how much time has changed, ✓ and compare them to their own parties. The 'Towers and Ramparts' feature would attract mainly a younger person because they might want to pretend they are really an archer from the medieval times. ✓

selection and comment

well-focused on the question

The words in this leaflet are used very effectively like, 'The kingmaker rallies his troops'. It speaks as though we are now in that time and it's happening right now ✓ and you are missing out if you're not there.

The first word in the 'Royal Weekend Party' section is 'Journey' and it makes the reader think they will be 'journeying' to another time.

attempts to probe the impact of specific words

Examiner comments

This is a thorough and detailed response, showing the student working methodically but quickly through the text, and linking comments to the details selected. There is a good focus on language and the range of comments and selection of detail would give this answer a good mark.

Question on how the text persuades: how to improve your answer

- To improve your answer always keep a clear focus on the question.
- Highlight key words in the question if you find it helpful. The key words in the question above are **persuade you to visit.**
- Make sure your answer covers all of the bullet points. Remember that in some texts content and language are probably more important than pictures and presentation.
- Try to link your comments with details from the text that support what you are saying.
- Do not give up after making one or two points. Choose a range of points to make about the content and look at three or four key words or phrases.
- The answer shows how to gain a really good mark by being methodical and linking details from the text to any comment you make.

Putting it into practice

On your own or with a partner explain what you now know about:

- identifying how a text attempts to persuade
- supporting your ideas by reference to the content of the text
- supporting your ideas by selecting and analysing key words and phrases
- identifying other techniques used to persuade.

In the future:

- you must practise this type of question using a range of texts
- use details and words/phrases to support your answer
- link the details from the text to a clear comment about how or why that detail would persuade the reader
- always work methodically through the text
- aim to produce a complete answer in 12–13 minutes.

Peer/Self-assessment activity

Now try to mark your answer to Activity I using the mark scheme below to help you.

 Improve your learning

8–10 marks
- Comments on how the text persuades and supports with details from the text.
- Better answers focus on the impact of words and phrases and how these help to persuade the reader.

5–7 marks
- Makes simple comments based on surface features of text.
- Shows awareness of the writer's different thoughts and feelings.
- Some focus on the question.

2–4 marks
- Very short, brief answers.
- Selects a few details but these are not linked to how the text persuades.

Your learning

This lesson will help you to:

- practise analysing persuasive writing
- develop a secure technique for answering this type of question.

When answering a persuasive writing question:

- track through the text methodically, so that you are clear about what the reader is being persuaded to do (to support a cause, donate money or time, buy something or visit somewhere)
- if there are bullet points in the question, use them to structure your answer
- focus on the content of the text and try to see the way language is used to persuade the reader
- if there are pictures/photographs, try to explain how they add to the persuasiveness of the whole text
- avoid vague or general comments: always focus on specific details.

Activity 1

Read the article opposite and answer the question below. The writer is trying to persuade the reader that whale hunting is still necessary for people living in the Faroe Islands, and that the picture of whale hunters as cruel and barbaric is far from the truth.

How does the writer defend whale hunting in the Faroe Islands? [10]

In your answer you should consider:

- *the details of life in the Faroe Islands*
- *the use of facts and figures*
- *the details of the hunt*
- *any other arguments the writer uses.*

Examiner tips

Remember the choice of words you can use instead of the writer 'says'.

- describes
- mentions
- tells
- suggests
- shows
- insists
- compares
- gives (details/examples)
- emphasises
- uses (examples/facts/statistics/quotations/irony/ humour/personal experience).

Whaling in the Faroe Islands

Ólavur lives in Leirvik, a village of 800 people in the Faroe Islands, where he teaches at the local primary school. But he is also a sheep farmer, a fisherman and a whaler. In the slatted shed next to his house, lamb, fish and whale meat hang drying in the wind. He gets his potatoes from his own patch. He has a modern house and a modern car. At least once a fortnight he and his family eat whale meat for dinner. They also eat the blubber together with dried fish.

[...]

Ólavur owns 10 sheep together with his mother-in-law. There are no slaughter-houses for sheep in the Faroes, and so he must slaughter and butcher them himself. 'Slaughtering is the worst job I know,' he says, 'but there's no alternative. Producing your own food obviously makes a big difference to the household budget, but it also gives you great satisfaction. Raising or catching what you eat yourself keeps you in touch with nature and keeps life interesting and varied. It also means a lot for community spirit in a small place like Leirvik. We talk about the sheep, we talk about fishing, and we talk about pilot whaling. We have it all in common.'

[...]

The Faroese have been catching pilot whales since the 10th century. [...] Since 1990, the annual catch of pilot whales has averaged about 1,000. With recent estimates putting the numbers of North Atlantic whales at 778,000, there can be no doubt that the pilot whale harvest is sustainable.

[...]

No one can predict when a school of pilot whales will appear close enough to land, in the right weather and sea conditions, for them to be herded ashore.

[...]

Boats drive the whales ashore, where they are killed with a deep incision behind the blowhole, severing the spinal cord and stopping the blood supply to the brain.

[...]

The preliminary results of recent veterinary monitoring of the killing techniques used incicate that on average a whale is unconscious within seconds of the cut being made, and dead in well under a minute. This makes killing in the pilot whale hunt as efficient as in any other form of hunting in Europe today.

Ólavur was about 17 years old when he killed his first whale. Young men are taught by their elders, usually their fathers or other relatives. 'I'm sure that no one who kills his own animals for food is unmoved by what he does. You want it done as quickly and with as little suffering as possible for the animal.' Given the circumstances under which pilot whaling is conducted, the knife is by far the most effective instrument for the job, while firearms are out of the question.

'I can well understand the strong reactions people have to pictures of pilot whaling in the Faroes,' says Ólavur. 'But all meat was once a living creature that someone had to kill so that it could end up on your plate. People seem to want to forget this fact of life.'

Peer/Self-assessment activity

1 Check your answers to Activity I.
- Did you use the bullet points to structure your answer?
- Did you work through the text in a clear sequence?
- Did you find evidence in the text to support your comments?
- Did you find any examples of particular words and phrases and link them to clear comments about how they persuade?

2 Now try to mark your answer to Activity I using the mark scheme below to help you.

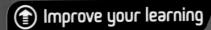

Improve your learning

8–10 marks
- Comments on how the text persuades and supports with details from the text.
- Better answers show clear understanding of the arguments made by the writer.

5–7 marks
- Makes simple comments based on surface features of the text.
- Shows some awareness of the writer's arguments.
- Some selection of details from the text.

2–4 marks
- Very short, brief answers.
- Selects a few details but these may not link to how the text persuades.

> ## Your learning
> ## This lesson will help you to:
> * learn how to compare and contrast two texts
> * understand how to approach this type of question.

The last question in the Reading exam paper involves you looking at and using material from two texts. You will be asked either to **compare and contrast** or to **make cross-references**.

If you are asked to **compare and contrast** this means you must look for similarities and differences in what the two texts are writing about. For example, one of the texts you read might be in support of foxhunting and the other text might be arguing against it. Your job in tackling the question might be to sort out the different views in each text and organise them into a paragraph.

If you are asked to **make cross-references**, this means you have to collect information from each text on a specific area of the text. For example, the two texts might both be about the same adventure holiday, and your job in tackling the question might be to collect the details from both texts and then write a paragraph that explains what activities a visitor could take part in.

Whichever type of question there is in the exam, **you must focus on the texts** and not what you think about the subject. You will waste time and get no marks if you ignore the question and simply give your views about the texts or the issues they discuss.

We will now look at each of the types of question in detail.

'Compare and contrast' questions

These questions ask you to look at the similarities and differences in what the two texts are writing about.

The wording of these questions may look like one of the following.

1 These two texts give very different impressions. In what ways are they different?
2 Compare and contrast what these two texts tell you about…
3 These two texts are about… Compare and contrast them using the following headings…

In this third type of question you will often be given a list of bullet points to follow, so that you can use them to structure to your answer. If you are told to organise your answer into paragraphs using the bullet points as headings, make sure you do exactly that. Remember that the examiner is trying to help you and you should take whatever help is offered.

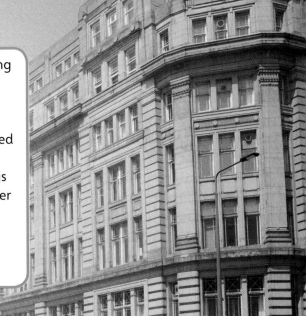

Examiner tips

- Comparing and contrasting is a skill that requires clear thinking and good organisation of material from the texts.
- Always read this question with extra care so that you know exactly what you are looking for in the two texts.
- If you are given bullet points, make sure your answer is focused on them; it is easy to drift off the question.
- You will find it helpful to use the bullet points as sub-headings for your answer. You will often be told to organise your answer into specific paragraphs, so make sure that you do.
- Your answer is likely to need to use specific details from the texts, so keep reminding yourself what the question is asking you, so the details you use are the right ones.

Activity 1

To begin with, it is important to be clear what each passage is about, before you work on comparing and contrasting what they have to say.

Read the Bradford brochure on pages 84–85 and the book extract on pages 86–87 and answer the first bullet point in the question below.

Both of these texts are about Bradford. One is from a brochure that tries to attract visitors, and the other is written by Bill Bryson who visited Bradford.

Compare what the two texts say about Bradford under the following headings:

- **the buildings**
- **the attractions in Bradford**
- **the places to eat. [10]**

1 Make a list of the ways the buildings are described in the two texts. One detail from each has been included to get you started.

Description of buildings in the Bradford brochure	Description of buildings in the book
'Stunning Victorian architecture'	'angular office buildings'

2 Work with a partner to compare and discuss your tables. How do the two texts describe the buildings? How are they different? Working together, and using the materials you have collected, write two or three sentences that show the differences or similarities in what each text says about the buildings.

3 You should repeat this activity for the other parts of the question and then move into answering the whole question in no more than 12–13 minutes, remembering that you should try to include the same level of detail from each text that you have done for the buildings section of the answer. If the two texts say similar things, don't be afraid to say that; where they show different things, aim to show the difference as clearly as you can.

Bradford

From stunning Victorian architecture to an amazing 3D visual feast at the IMAX Cinema, Bradford is culturally rich with a city centre full of history, yet vibrant and cosmopolitan. Two hundred years ago Bradford changed from a small rural town, whose people spun wool and wove cloth, into the wool capital of the world. Bradford now enjoys a fantastic architectural legacy from this period, a heritage that can be explored through a series of self guided trails available from the Tourist Information Centre.

Many exceptional historic buildings remain, including the Grade 1 listed City Hall (built 1873), the gothic style Wool Exchange (1867), and the 15th century cathedral. Bradford's history is evident in the popular Bradford Industrial Museum in the unique commercial area known as Little Germany.

There are plenty of modern attractions to capture the imagination. The award winning National Media Museum – five floors of interactive displays – charts the past, present and future of image making and has three cinemas, including the incredible IMAX experience with its giant 3D screen.

Other major attractions within the city include Cartwright Hall Art Gallery, set in beautiful Lister Park, voted Britain's best park in 2006; the Alhambra Theatre; and The Priestley Theatre. There is a packed programme of festivals and events, including three major film festivals and the world-famous Bradford Festival – two weeks of music, theatre, film and street events.

Those who prefer shopping will also love Bradford, as the city is home to a host of unusual speciality shops, markets and mill shops where many bargains can be found.

In the city, high street names rub shoulders with local shops, and for an elegant upmarket shopping excursion outside the city, nearby Ilkley offers top quality shops from high fashion to fine chocolatiers.

The city's nightlife, with its rich variety of restaurants, bars and nightclubs, might surprise you. And discover for yourself why Bradford has been crowned UK Curry capital, with well over 200 Asian restaurants across the district. But Bradford also has an interesting mix of fine international cuisine and traditional Yorkshire fare. The city has many traditional pubs to enjoy, like the New Beehive Inn with its Edwardian interior and gas lit bars, which caters for the Real Ale enthusiast, and appears regularly in the Good Beer Guide.

Plus ...

In June, Bradford swings to the sounds of the festival with live music in Centenary Square. By night, take in a show at the magnificent Alhambra Theatre.

The Industrial Museum gears up daily for a public demonstration of its Motive Power engines at 10.30 am and 2.00 pm (most days).

Odsal Stadium is home to Rugby League's 2005 Super League champions, Bradford Bulls, while football takes centre stage across town at Valley Parade, the home of Bradford City. There's fun for all the family at Bradford's 11 public swimming pools, and some of the other sports facilities include ten-pin bowling in the city centre and ice skating at the ever-popular Bradford Ice Arena.

The National Media Museum has three diverse film festivals each year – The Bradford Film Festival (March), 'Bite the Mango' Film Festival (Sept) and The Bradford Animation Festival (Oct/Nov) – perfect for film lovers of all ages!

Bradford

Bradford's role in life is to make every place else in the world look better in comparison, and it does this very well. Nowhere on my trip around Britain would I see a more depressing city. Nowhere would I pass more vacant shops, their windows covered with tattered posters for pop concerts, or more office buildings covered with TO LET signs. At least one shop in three in the town centre was empty, and most of the rest seemed to be barely hanging on.

Once the town had one of the greatest collections of Victorian architecture anywhere, but you would scarcely guess it now. Scores of wonderful buildings were swept away to make room for wide new roads and angular office buildings. Nearly everything in the city suffers from well-intentioned but misguided meddling by planners.

Nowadays, the local authorities are desperately trying to promote their meagre stock of old buildings. In a modest cluster of narrow streets just out of the city centre there still stand some three dozen large and striking warehouses, mostly built between 1860 and 1874, which together make up the area known as Little Germany. Of all the once thriving wool precincts in the city, only the few dark buildings of Little Germany survive in any number, and even this promising small neighbourhood seems bleak. At the time of my visit, two-thirds of the buildings were covered in scaffolding, and the other third had TO LET signs on them.

Still, Bradford is not without its charms. Lister Park is very attractive, there are some good pubs, and The Alhambra Theatre, built in 1914, has been skilfully renovated and remains the most wonderful place to see a pantomime.

The National Media Museum has brought a welcome flicker of life to a corner of the city where previously you only had the world's most appalling indoor ice rink to go to. As I had an hour to kill, I walked over to the Museum and had a look through the various galleries. I watched in wonder as throngs of people parted with substantial sums of cash to see the two o'clock IMAX show. I've been to these IMAX screenings before, and frankly I can't understand the appeal. I know the screen is massive and the visual representation stunning, but the films are always so incredibly dull.

I forgot to mention curry houses in my brief list of Bradford's glories, which was a terrible oversight. Bradford may have lost a wool trade but it has gained a thousand excellent Indian restaurants, which I personally find a reasonable swap as I have a strictly limited need for bales of wool, but can take about as much Indian food as you care to shovel at me.

The oldest of the Bradford curry houses, I'm told, and certainly one of the best and cheapest, is the Kashmir, just up the road from the Alhambra. For £5 I had a small feast that was rich, delicious, and so hot that it made my fillings sizzle.

Afterwards, bloated and with a stomach bubbling away like a heated beaker in a mad-scientist movie, I stepped out into the Bradford evening and wondered what to do with myself. It was just six o'clock on a Saturday evening, but the place felt dead.

Here are two student responses to the exam task below. Read the answers and the examiner comments.

Both of these texts are about Bradford. One is from a brochure that tries to attract visitors, and the other is written by Bill Bryson who visited Bradford.

Compare what the two texts say about Bradford under the following headings:
- the buildings
- the attractions in Bradford
- the places to eat. [10]

Extract typical of a F grade answer

Student 1

weak response

In the Bradford brochure some of the buildings remain and in Bryson's article it is a very depressing city.

loses the focus on buildings

The attractions in the Bradford brochure is that it has more attractive things and more things to do, ✓ but in the article he says it is disgusting, and everything is tatty and with nothing to do. ✓

In the brochure it says there are restaurants, bars and nightclubs and Bradford has been crowned UK Curry capital with 200 Asian restaurants ✓ across the district. And in the article he says for £5 you can have a feast of as much food as you want ✓ but he doesn't like the food. He says it's a terrible oversight.

misunderstands

no! Incorrect reading

Examiner comments

This is a weak response. The student loses the focus on the first of the bullet points and gains no reward. The second paragraph lacks specific detail but is aware of the contrast of views in the two texts, and though there is some reward for selection of detail in the third paragraph, there is also a misreading of Bryson's viewpoint.

Student 2

Bill Bryson says there was a lot of scaffolding around so this meant there was a lot of new building going on. There were a lot of 'To Let' signs and many places were vacant. ✓ The brochure says there are a lot ✓ of old buildings that tells the history of Bradford. There are a lot of new buildings that have just been built and most of the buildings are award-winning.

Bill Bryson says there are some good pubs in the city and he thinks Lister Park is very attractive ✓ and the National Media Museum has brought a welcome flicker of life. The brochure says the city is rich and full of history. They have plenty of sports halls and museums. ✓ There is fun for all the family ✓ and it says how great the museum is with its giant 3D screen. It also has a lot of festivals ✓ like the Bradford Festival and the three film festivals. The brochure tells you when the festivals take place. There is also perfect shopping with speciality shops and markets.

Bill Bryson says you can get a small feast for £5 in the Kasmir curry house ✓ and it is rich and delicious. He says there are excellent Indian curry houses. ✓ The brochure says Bradford has been crowned UK Curry capital ✓ with well over 200 Asian restaurants and they have a rich variety of restaurants. They say Bradford has an interesting mix of fine international cuisine ✓ and traditional Yorkshire fare.

Examiner comments

This is a thorough and detailed response to the question. Notice how much use the student makes of the text to support the conflicting views expressed in the two texts, and the way the answer has a neat balance of overview and specific detail.

Comparing and contrasting texts: how to improve your response

As you have seen with these examples of students' work, to improve your response you must read the question carefully and do exactly what it tells you to do. The bullet points demanded very specific details, in response:

- Student 1 offers almost no detail from the text until the final part of the answer
- Student 2 shows exactly how this type of question should be answered, with lots of detail but also making contrasts between the texts. This answer showed the value of keeping a clear focus on the question and making good use of the details in the texts in the answer.

Putting it into practice

On your own or with a partner explain what you now know about:

- making comparisons and contrasts across two texts
- supporting your ideas by reference to the texts
- organising and presenting your answer
- what makes the difference between typical grade F and C responses.

In the future:

- you must practise this type of question using a range of texts
- always follow the instructions in the question
- make sure you focus clearly on what the bullet points ask for
- look for similarities but also differences
- aim to produce a complete answer in 12–13 minutes.

'Cross-reference' questions

Your learning

This lesson will help you to:

- learn how to find information from two texts
- understand how to approach this type of question.

This type of question asks you to find information from two texts.

- This means that you must focus on what you have been asked to find.
- It is also important to identify in your answer which text the information came from.

Examiner tips

- This type of question does not involve your opinions. You should not get involved in the issues.
- Focus on what the question asks you to do, and nothing else.

Activity 1

Read the article opposite and the web pages on pages 92–93.

1 Make a list of the things that are said about the accommodation at Astley Woods in the two texts. One detail from each has been included in the table below to get you started.

What is said about the accommodation in the article	What is said about the accommodation on the web pages
'New Forest' chalets have DVDs, hot tubs and their own parking places	'New Forest' chalets have en-suite bathrooms and saunas

2 Work with a partner to compare and discuss your tables. What do the two texts say about the accommodation? How are they similar or different? Working together, and using the materials you have collected, write two or three sentences that show the differences or similarities in what each text says about the accommodation at Astley Woods.

Activity 2

1 On your own or working with a partner, and building on your work for Activity I, note down the relevant information in each extract to answer the question below:

Both of these texts are about adventure holidays at Astley Woods. Compare and contrast them under the following headings:

- **the accommodation at Astley Woods**
- **the restaurants at Astley Woods**
- **the Astley Woods settings. [10]**

Astley Woods – holiday review

The appeal of Astley Woods is that it is 'in the wild'. Actually, their sites are pretty much in the middle of nowhere, though this is sold as an attraction because you can 'get away from it all'. To be fair, the site we visited was set in glorious woodland with lots of nature trails and plenty of wildlife to try and spot.

There are number of choices in accommodation to suit your budget. At the bottom of the price range is the 'Wychwood Forest' chalet, up to the most expensive 'New Forest' chalets that have things like a DVD in the cabin, private parking, and their own hot tub. The chalets are not the most attractive wooden buildings, but ours was clean and homely, although I heard one visitor complain that her chalet had a fusty smell and had dirty marks on the walls and doors. On arrival one of the first things I recommend is getting down to the Woods Market, which is a reasonably priced, well-stocked shop that sells freshly baked goods and the range of food that you're likely to find in small supermarkets.

One of the problems with Astley Woods is that it can get quite expensive, depending on what you want to do. It's true that it can be a relatively cheap week if you're happy just going to the pool, walking round the site and eating in. However, if you want to try your hand at the kinds of activities that are on offer, they do not come cheap. For example, quad biking was £35 for an hour and massages were £30 for 30 minutes. Activities I would recommend are the horse riding lessons and the archery, which I really enjoyed, but it's advisable to book activities in advance, because the popular ones get booked up very quickly.

There's lots to do and many of the activities are suitable for children or those with families. You can also hire bikes, and it was good to be able to cycle all around the site and on the nature trails, though I thought £22 each for a bike (Mon–Fri) was very expensive. Another problem was that the bikes all looked similar so do try to remember where you park – one day I spent half an hour looking round trying to find my bike.

One annoying thing for me about the two Astley Woods centres I visited was that they seemed to be constantly under construction. I imagine this is kept to a minimum in peak season but as a visitor going in the cheap season I found various problems such as roads in the centre closed off, and for two days the pool was shut down for maintenance.

The restaurants have varied menus and plenty of choices, but they are all quite expensive. One of the complaints I heard from visitors was that the restaurants often seemed to be under-staffed, and there were grumbles about slow service.

So is it worth it? Well, if you love swimming and hanging about a pool I suppose it is pretty good. Walking or cycling round the park is enjoyable except for all the noisy people which doesn't quite match the tranquil image presented in the Astley Woods brochure. Overall, it is probably worth going to one of the centres for a few days away if you have never been before, and it's good if you have children and are willing to pay – quite a lot – for some of the extra things on offer. Having done it once though, I'm not sure I'd go back.

Astley Woods 'Action Plus' Holidays

Why choose an Astley Woods 'Action Plus' Holiday? Maybe you want a holiday that pushes you to the limit. Or you have children who enjoy trying their hand at new, exciting activities. An 'Action Plus' holiday delivers excitement and challenge for all. But if you would rather enjoy more gentle pursuits in locations of wonderful natural beauty, Astley Woods holiday centres can offer that too. Enjoy the breeze when you sail across the lake, or join one of our woodland walks with our friendly Tracker Guides. And if you are looking for more challenge, you could always try the Log Swing, the High Tree Trek or the Zip Wire Challenge.

Whatever you want from a holiday, Astley Woods works tirelessly to offer 'Action Plus' holidays that will leave you with the warm glow of personal achievement and of time well spent in beautiful natural surroundings.

Astley Woods also provides superb accommodation for your holiday. We offer our standard 'Wychwood Forest' chalets for guests who simply want to enjoy the huge range of facilities available at our sites. For guests who want to be pampered, we offer our 'New Forest' chalets which are exclusively designed and stylishly furnished to the highest standards, and include en-suite bathrooms and saunas.

Children's 'Action Plus' Holidays

At Astley Woods we know that children learn best while they're having fun. That's why we have created a fantastic range of activities for children in every age group, and all of them are run by expert, qualified staff.

You can watch your children taking part in new activities, making new friends and learning new skills – and you are welcome to join in as much, or as little, as you'd like to. Or you can have some well-earned time to yourself, knowing that your children are in the safe, dependable hands of our staff.

Astley Woods Family Holidays

With their location, in 300 acres of unspoilt natural forest, the Astley Woods holiday centres offer a great choice of outdoor activities for all the family and for groups of all ages. We have something for everyone: from horse-riding to archery and from bird-watching to canoeing. Our instructors are all highly qualified and will help build your confidence and skill, whether you're an expert or beginner, ensuring your enjoyment whatever activity you choose.

We know that after a day spent exploring, playing or just relaxing, you'll want to enjoy a family meal together. We offer a range of superb restaurants and bistros where you can do just that, re-living the experiences of the day in a relaxed atmosphere. Each of our centres has a variety of themed restaurants, and with menus from every continent, we're sure that you'll feel spoilt for choice.

Memories to hold forever

Can you remember your own family holidays as a child: carefree, full of fun and memories that last forever? Let us help to create those experiences for all the family. The stunning forest locations and the magic of nature become the backdrop for family memories that will last a lifetime.

A Children's 'Action Plus' holiday will give all the family the opportunity to spend precious time together, as well as offering your children a range of supervised activities that will mean they'll never get bored the whole time they're with us. We also make sure that whilst they are enjoying themselves, you can have time for yourself, either to make the most of the facilities on offer, or to just relax in the delightful surroundings.

Whether it's inside or outdoors, your children will have plenty of activities to choose from. Outside, they can enjoy the soccer schools, abseiling and paintballing, whilst inside there are activities like fashion-design, movie-making and DJing. Every age and interest is catered for and because our emphasis is firmly on safety and on fun, you can be sure that you can relax when they are letting off steam.

There's so much more to keep them entertained at Astley Woods holiday centres than they could ever manage to do in just a single visit, so they're sure to pester you for another visit. We hope you'll share their wish to return again and again.

GradeStudio

Here are two student responses to the exam task below. Read the answers and examiner comments.

Both of these texts are about adventure holidays at Astley Woods. Compare and contrast them under the following headings:

- the accommodation at Astley Woods
- the restaurants at Astley Woods
- the Astley Woods settings. [10]

Student 1

Accommodation
Both of the texts say about the two types of chalet – the 'Wychwood Forest' and the 'New Forest' chalets ✓ but in the article the writer says some people think they are quite smelly and dirty. ✓

Restaurants
The article says the restaurants are expensive ✓ if you go to eat in them but the web page brochure says they are places where families can enjoy a meal together, ✓ but some families could not afford expensive meals, so the article might be more true.

Settings
Both the article and the web page brochure say that the settings are very nice and in the woods. ✓

Examiner comments

The student organises the answer so that each part of the question is covered, but in each case there is more to say, and this would have gained the student additional marks. The more detail you can include in your answer, the better your mark will be.

Using information from two texts: how to improve your response

To improve your answer you must refer to both texts and select the relevant points clearly. The evidence needs to be chosen carefully, making sure that it is always focused on what you have been asked to do.

- Notice that the first answer is just too thin and brief, especially towards the end.
- The second answer goes up the grades because it uses a good range of detail from both texts and almost nothing is missed.

Student 2

Accommodation

Both pieces tell the reader about the types of chalet at Astley Woods, the 'Wychwood Forest' and 'New Forest' chalets, ✓ but whereas the article says the 'New Forest' ones have DVDs, private parking and hot tubs, ✓ the web page brochure says they have en-suite bathrooms and saunas. ✓ The writer of the article says they are OK but not very attractive. ✓

Restaurants

The web page brochure says their restaurants are 'superb' ✓ and that they are good for a family meal in a 'relaxed atmosphere' ✓ and it says there are lots of different meals to choose from. However, the article said the food was expensive ✓ and the service there was not good because 'there were grumbles about slow service'. ✓

Settings

The web page brochure talks about the centres being in 'locations of wonderful natural beauty' ✓ and later says they are in '300 acres of unspoilt natural forest', ✓ which makes them sound good places to visit. 'The writer of the article also liked the site, 'set in glorious woodland with lots of nature trails', ✓ but also says the sites are 'in the middle of nowhere' ✓ so they might be hard to get to if you don't have a car.

Examiner comments

This is a confident and assured response from a student who knows exactly what to do. The details are well selected. Each of the questions is covered thoroughly.

Putting it into practice

On your own or with a partner explain what you now know about:
- finding information across two texts
- supporting your ideas by reference to the texts
- organising and presenting your answer
- what makes the difference between typical E and C grade answers.

In the future:
- you must practise this type of question using a range of texts
- always follow the instructions in the question
- make sure you focus only on what you are asked to do
- look for similarities but also differences
- select and use examples from the texts but do not overdo it
- aim to produce a complete answer in 12–13 minutes.

2 Writing information and ideas

What will the Writing paper look like?

In this paper you have one hour for two pieces of transactional writing. 'Transactional' means writing that pays special attention to audience, purpose and format. You will produce two pieces of writing, for example: a letter, a report, an article, a leaflet, a speech/talk or a review.

The paper tests your writing skills. Both answers will be marked out of 20.

- You will be marked out of 13 for what you say and the organisation of your work.
- You will be marked out of 7 for sentence structure, punctuation and spelling.

What will the questions be like?

The questions will test your ability to do some of the following:

- argue a case
- explain something
- persuade someone to do something
- give advice
- comment on an issue
- write a review.

The two tasks will require you to do different things and may test different skills.

What should I do?

- Read the instructions carefully; they are there to help you.
- Divide your time equally; about 30 minutes per question.
- Make sure that your answers are close to the length suggested.
- Read the questions carefully and make sure that you answer the question you are being asked.
- You will be given some bullet points to help you approach the task. Make sure you follow the bullet points.
- Plan what you will say in your introduction, in each paragraph and in the conclusion.
- Think carefully about your audience before you start to write.
- When you have finished writing, read through your work and check for errors. Make changes if they will improve your work.

How will I be assessed?

The examiner will assess your answers against the assessment criteria outlined on page v.

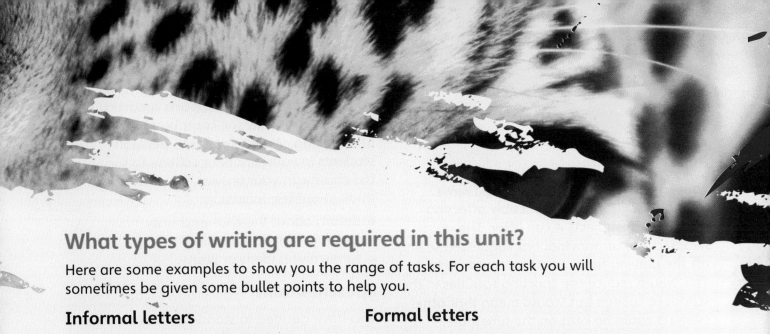

What types of writing are required in this unit?

Here are some examples to show you the range of tasks. For each task you will sometimes be given some bullet points to help you.

Informal letters

Your grandparents are not keen on email or the phone. They like proper letters written by their grandchildren. They have asked you to suggest Christmas presents for your younger brother and sister. Write a friendly letter suggesting the kind of gifts your brother and sister would like. In your answer you may like to think about the following:

- a friendly introduction
- possible presents for your brother with reasons
- possible presents for your sister with reasons
- a friendly conclusion.

Formal letters

You have read a letter in your local newspaper suggesting that all teenagers are rude, lazy and poorly educated. Write your reply to this letter. In your reply you may like to think about the following:

- a general introduction referring to the original letter
- occasions when young people could be considered to be rude, lazy and poorly educated
- occasions when young people are not
- the kind of pressures young people are under in education
- things that young people do in the community
- a concluding paragraph.

Reports

Your school or college has received news that it must cut its costs, possibly affecting the range of subjects it can offer. The headteacher or principal has suggested selling off the playing fields to a supermarket chain. This would reduce the sporting facilities in the school or college but would mean that other subjects could be kept on the timetable.

You, as representative of the students, have been asked to write a report on the matter for your headteacher/principal. Write the report. In your answer, you may like to think about the following:

- an introduction, stating your view
- advantages of selling the playing field
- disadvantages of selling the playing field
- your conclusion.

Articles for newspapers and magazines

The government has decided that all students must stay in full-time education until they are 18, either in school or in a further education college. You have been asked to write an article for a local newspaper stating your views on this decision. Write the article. In your answer, you may like to think about the following:

- reasons why it is a good idea to stay on in education
- reasons why it is not a good idea
- your personal view.

Leaflets

Your school or college supports a particular charity but recently the contributions have been falling. Write a leaflet to persuade students in your school or college to support the charity. In your answer, you may like to think about the following:

- details about the chosen charity
- why it is worth supporting
- fund-raising ideas or plans.

Speeches/talks

You have decided to stand for the school or college council. Write the speech you will give to your year group to persuade them to vote for you. In your answer you may like to think about the following:

- introducing yourself
- aspects of the school you would hope to change
- why the students should vote for you.

Reviews

A teenage magazine has asked you to review a book, film, television programme or CD. Write a review which will give your audience a clear idea of the qualities and weaknesses of the subject you have chosen. In your answer you may like to think about the following:

- details about your book, film, television programme or CD
- aspects about it you enjoyed
- things that you felt were weak or poor
- an evaluation and recommendation.

What will I learn about transactional writing?

You will learn about:

- the different transactional writing tasks – letters, reports, newspaper and magazine articles, leaflets, speeches and reviews
- how to lay out/format each type of writing on the page
- the need to adopt the right tone in your writing
- how to choose the right kind of content
- some different ways of approaching the tasks
- how to think about your audience and purpose.

In transactional writing the emphasis is on audience and purpose, and, in some cases, format. So what do we mean by these three things?

Audience

This means the person or people you are writing to or for.

Purpose

This means the reason for the piece of writing – for example, to argue a point of view, to persuade, to comment/explain or review.

Format

Format means how you set something out.

2.1 Informal letters

Your learning

This lesson will help you to:

- organise and lay out an informal letter correctly
- write with an informal style and tone.

What do you need to know about informal letters?

- **Audience:** often to friends and family.
- **Purpose:** to keep in touch, to send information, give advice.
- **Language:** informal.
- **Tone:** friendly, chatty.

If you write an informal letter in the exam, you will:

- be told what your letter is about
- be given an address, or told to use your own
- need to lay out your letter as shown opposite
- need to plan and organise your letter as shown.

Activity 1

Read the letter and comments opposite. These show you the features of an informal letter. The student was asked to write a letter to a friend about where to go on holiday together.

1. Try writing your own informal letter. Read the task below, set for an exam.

> **Your grandparents are not keen on email or the phone. They like proper letters written by their grandchildren. They have asked you to suggest Christmas presents for your younger brother and sister.**
>
> **Write a friendly letter suggesting the kind of gifts your brother and sister would like. [20]**
>
> *You may like to think about the following in your letter:*
> - *a friendly introduction*
> - *presents for your brother with reasons*
> - *presents for your sister with reasons*
> - *a friendly conclusion.*

2. Plan the informal letter you will write. It needs to be one and a half to two sides long. Use the letter opposite and the notes below to help you.

- Plan four paragraphs: one for each bullet point above. Note down what you will say in each one.
- Use a friendly tone: for example, 'It was great to see you at the weekend'.
- Make the letter personal. Refer to things that your grandparents and you both know or have experienced: for example, family pets.
- Give advice: remember this is the purpose of the letter.

3. Now write your letter. Use your plan to help you. Use the format shown opposite.

Your address → 4 Brown Road
Sheffield
S22 4BD

Greeting/salutation

The date → 5 September 2010

Dear Chloe,

I've got all the information we need to make a decision about where to go for our hard earned holiday and I've put it in this letter. The email has crashed and so I thought it would be simplest just to send you the lot. I can't wait for the exams to be over. All this revision is sending me mad.

Anyway, we could go to one of three places. The first one is Brighton. This has a good nightlife and the beach for lazy days while we recover. It's not far to go either.

The second is camping in that site we went to with our parents a couple of years ago in Anglesey. This would be cheap but you know how uncomfortable those camp beds are and we would have to have someone to take us and pick us up. I can't see the night life as being too exciting!

Then there is that cheap holiday in Spain. This would be great, lots of sun and swimming but can you see our parents letting us go by ourselves?

Three or four middle paragraphs covering the points you want to make. Make sure you cover each bullet point in the task

So what do you think? I really want to go to Brighton. You know how much I like lying in the sun topping up the tan. You can always go jogging along the beach if you want to keep up your fitness routine! I think you'll be too tired though after all that dancing. Anyway, let me know.

Final paragraph to round off and reinforce the purpose of the letter, and what you want your friend to do next

Give me a ring when you've read all the information. Can't wait to see you again. Best of luck with the exams!

Lots of love,

Informal closure

Clare

Your first name

Examiner tips

- Remember that you have 30 minutes to complete this task.
- Read the question carefully.
- Plan your answer before you start writing.
- Lay out your letter correctly. You will get more marks.
- Never use text language in your letters. You will lose marks if you do.
- One-third of your marks is for sentence structure, punctuation and spelling. Check and correct your work!

Here is a student response to the exam task below. Read the answer and the examiner comments.

Your grandparents are not keen on email or the phone. They like proper letters written by their grandchildren. They have asked you to suggest Christmas presents for your younger brother and sister. Write a friendly letter suggesting the kind of gifts your brother or sister would like. [20]

Student 1

14 Maytree Road
Knutsford
Cheshire

Dear nan,

I now I havent seen you in a while so I thought I will write you a letter even thou I am no good at spelling and you will probley see some mistakes in my letter. Its unlucky you have no email because then I would of sent you some emails insted of writing this letter enyway, how are you, I heard that you went to spain for the week but you havnt sent us eny pictures. Im OK, my work experience was great and our holiday was good. Peter was being a bit of a pain but I servived.

Enyway, hear are some toys you could think of bying Peter. he's five now and he's well into football and I'd buy him a new football, if I was you, he likes power rangers as well and one of those would be a good idea. Just think of what you bort me when I was his age and you wont go wrong.

Enyway I hope you will write back to me and come round my house and I mite come round to your's.

I have to go now, got to do my English homework. I will see you when I can

Lots of love
your grandson
Jake Philips

Examiner comments

Content and organisation

Strong points

- The style is pleasant and friendly.
- Most of the format is correct but it needs a postcode and date.

Weak points

- The student has not thought about his audience. His Nan would know the age of his brother and his own surname.
- The student hasn't included ideas for presents for his sister.
- There is not much variety in the vocabulary used.
- The student has spent too long on the chatty introduction and does not spend enough time on the actual advice to his Nan.
- The ending ('your grandson') is a little too formal.

Sentence structure, punctuation and spelling

Strong points

- The letter is paragraphed.

Weak points

- Lots of sentences begin in the same way. For example, a number begin with 'Enyway'.
- The following words were misspelled by the student: 'instead', 'survived', 'anyway', 'buying'.
- Commas are used where full stops are needed. (For example, in the first paragraph.)
- The student made errors in apostrophe usage. For example, 'haven't', 'I'm', 'yours'.
- Some words ('Spain', 'Nan') need to have capital letters.

Informal letters: how to improve your response

- Use the proper format.
- Use paragraphs to arrange your work.
- Use a friendly tone.
- Keep in sight why you are writing the letter.
- Think carefully about who is reading your letter.
- Be interesting!
- Use a variety of sentence types.
- Take great care with your spelling and punctuation.
- Check and correct your work at the end.

Putting it into practice

Working in pairs, look at the letters you and your partner have written in response to Activity 1 on page 100.

Compare your responses.
- Do they fulfil the task?
- Do they have an appropriate friendly style?
- Have you both got the format correct?
- What are the good features in each response?
- Are the spelling and punctuation correct?
- Are paragraphs used?

Peer/Self-assessment activity

Can you note down at least one strong point and one thing to improve in your letter for each heading below:
- content
- organisation
- sentence structure
- punctuation
- spelling?

Your learning

This lesson will help you to:

- practise an exam task on an informal letter
- develop a secure approach to writing an informal letter.

When writing an informal letter remember it is important to think about your audience and purpose and use the right kind of tone.

Activity 1

Write your own informal letter in response to the exam task below.

Your older sister has gone abroad to a place where email and telephone contact are impossible. Write her a letter in which you tell her some family news but also try to persuade her to come home. [20]

You may like to include:

- *recent news from home*
- *reasons why you would like her to come back home*
- *how much you and your family miss her*
- *any other aspects that you feel are important.*

Examiner tips

- Remember that you have 30 minutes to complete this task.
- Plan what you are going to say before you start writing.
- Use the correct format. Check back to pages 100–101 if you are unsure about this.
- Make the letter real to you by thinking about an actual person that you could be writing to.
- Take care to use 'I' and not 'i'.
- Do not use multiple punctuation marks such as '!!!!' or '???'.

Peer/Self-assessment activity

I Check your answer to Activity I. Use the mark scheme on pages 106–107.

- Did you set out your letter in the right way?
- Is there an introduction to the topic?
- Are the central paragraphs clearly organised into topics?
- Did you cover each bullet point?
- Does it sound like a letter that would be sent to an older sister?
- Would she find it interesting?
- Have you checked your punctuation and spelling and that you have used a variety of sentence structures? Correct any mistakes.
- How could you improve your letter?

Content and organisation (13 marks)

Typical D grade answer

- You know exactly what you are being asked to do in your writing.
- You know exactly who you are writing for and have thought about what will interest that person or group.
- Your work is long enough and you have covered a number of points in detail.
- Your writing has paragraphs and the structure makes sense.
- You have used a good variety of carefully chosen words.
- You have thought carefully about why you are writing, and about for whom you are writing, and have adapted your style to suit it.
- You have got all the details of the appropriate audience correct.

Typical E grade answer

- You have some idea of what you are supposed to be writing about.
- Your layout is partially correct, but could be improved.
- You have begun to give some evidence or support for what you are writing.
- You have given some structure to what you are writing so that your work makes some sense.
- You have begun to think about what will interest your audience.
- Your vocabulary is not limited to simple words.

Typical G grade answer

- Some of the work shows you know who you are writing for and there is a little formatting.
- You show only a very limited understanding of how to write for a particular audience.
- Your work is too short and not all of it is relevant to the task.
- Your ideas are mostly in a sensible order.
- You use a couple of paragraphs but you do not show much understanding of how a paragraph should be used.
- The way you have written does not show much evidence that you know who you are writing for.
- Your range of vocabulary is rather limited. You are only using simple words.

Sentence structure, punctuation and spelling (7 marks)

Typical C grade answer

- You use lots of different kinds of sentences and sentence openings.

- You have made very few, if any, mistakes with your full stops, commas and apostrophes.

- You make very few, if any, spelling mistakes.

- You keep to one tense and you do not make mistakes with subject/verb agreement. You use a singular verb with a singular subject and a plural verb with a plural subject.

Typical E grade answer

- You have used a number of different sentence openings and structures.

- Most of your punctuation is correct though you may have made one or two mistakes with full stops, commas and apostrophes.

- Most of your spelling, even of more difficult words, is correct.

- Generally you keep to one tense and you do not make mistakes with subject/verb agreement. You use a singular verb with a singular subject and a plural verb with a plural subject.

Typical G grade answer

- You have only used very simple sentence structures.

- You have made a number of mistakes in the way you have used commas, full stops and apostrophes.

- Most of your spelling is correct but you make mistakes with simple words.

- You have not been consistent in your tenses and sometimes you have, for example, used a singular verb with a plural subject (for example, 'We was going').

Your learning

This lesson will help you to:

- write a formal letter correctly
- understand key differences between formal and informal letters.

What do you need to know about formal letters?

- **Audience:** often to a person you do not know, or know in a more formal way. It could be an employer, council official, newspaper editor or head teacher.
- **Purpose:** could be to apply for a job, give a view on an issue of concern, complain.
- **Language:** formal, polite. Don't use slang expressions. You need to impress.
- **Tone:** fairly serious, not chatty. Never be aggressive or rude.

If you write a formal letter in the exam:

- you will be told what your letter is about
- you may be given addresses, otherwise you must make them up
- you will need to lay out your letter as shown opposite
- you will need to plan and organise your letter as shown opposite.

Activity 1

Read the formal letter and comments opposite. These show you the features of a formal letter. The student was asked to write a letter to the Children's Services Department about the lack of play areas for children in the city.

1 Try writing your own formal letter. Read the task below, set for an exam.

> **The quiet road where you live is increasingly used by cars and lorries to avoid congestion on the nearby main road. As they are driving fast, you are worried about the safety of your family. You feel that the county/town council should install traffic calming devices to protect your and others' families.**

Write the letter you would send to the council to ask them to install suitable traffic calming devices. [20]

You may like to think about:

- *your own family situation*
- *the dangers and problems caused by the increased traffic*
- *the measures you feel should be taken to slow the traffic down.*

2 Work with a partner. Plan the formal letter you will write. It needs to be one and a half to two sides long. Use the letter opposite to help you.

The name and address of the person you are writing to. If you know the name of the person you are writing to you should use that, if not then write the person's title

Address you are writing from. This will usually be your own address

Date

15 Link Street
Liverpool
L15 7XP

29 September 2010

The Manager
Children's Services Department
Liverpool City Council
Liverpool
L1 1AB

The name of the person you are writing to. Again, if you know the name use it, if not use an appropriate title

Dear Sir or Madam

I am writing, as a concerned mother of a three-year-old, to request that we have more play areas for children in the city. At present, many children have no green areas close to where they live which means that they get very little exercise.

I am living with my toddler daughter in a flat in one of the high rise blocks near the city centre and the flat is not big enough for my daughter to run around in and get enough exercise.

Three or four paragraphs developing the main point and arguing for more play facilities

The nearest park to where I live is more than a mile away and my daughter finds it hard to walk so far. I can watch her play in the street at the bottom of the block of flats but she hurts herself if she falls on the hard concrete and the road is close by.

I have talked about this to other mothers in the flats and we all agree that the council needs to provide children with a safe play area closer to where we live. We are told all the time that children become too fat if they don't exercise enough and yet there is no place near where my daughter can run around.

I should be grateful if you could take my points into consideration when the council next meets. I look forward to hearing from you.

Yours faithfully,

Diane Smith (Mrs)

Formal closure. Yours sincerely (for a named addressee); Yours faithfully (for a unnamed addressee)

Your full name, and title if appropriate

Examiner tips

In a task like this it is often a good idea to imagine that you are the person writing the letter, in this case a mother or father with small children, rather than a student writing at school.

GradeStudio

Here is a student response to the exam task below. Read the answer and the examiner comments.

The quiet road where you live is increasingly used by cars and lorries to avoid congestion on the nearby main road. As they are driving fast, you are worried about the safety of your family. You feel that the county/town council should install traffic calming devices to protect your and others' families.

Write the letter you would send to the council to ask them to install suitable traffic calming devices. [20]

Extract typical of a C grade answer

Student 1

47 Holly Road
Salisbury
Wiltshire
SP21 1AA
28th March 2010

The Manager
Transport Department
Wiltshire County Council
Trowbridge
Wiltshire

Dear Sir,

I am extremely worried about the speed of traffic down the street I live in. I am a mother of two small children and I fear that they and others living in the street could be seriously hurt by the thoughtless behaviour of drivers using Holly Road as a way of avoiding the congestion on the main road. There seems to be a constant stream of cars and lorries rushing down our street and it is an accident waiting to happen.

There has to be some way of controlling the amount of traffic and its speed. I have talked to my neighbours and we are all agreed that we should have a 20 mile per hour speed limit with speed cameras, this could slow the traffic down a bit and may put people off using our street which was never meant to have heavy traffic on it.

I think it is time the council thought about this because I am afraid for the safety of my children and I know others feel the same way. Could you please look into this and send someone down to check the amount of traffic and its speed so that something can be done before someone is killed?

Yours faithfully,

Jessica Collins (Mrs)

Examiner comments

Content and organisation

Strong points

- The letter has the correct format.
- The student has a sound understanding of the purpose of the letter.
- They have understood what the town/county council can do.
- The letter uses paragraphs.
- The tone is polite and thoughtful.
- The content is suitably detailed.
- The student has thought about a real situation – a mother of two children.
- Possible solutions to the problem are carefully explained.

Sentence structure, punctuation and spelling

Strong points

- Punctuation is generally correct.
- There is a variety of sentence structures and sentence openings.
- Spelling is mostly accurate.

Weak points

- Sometimes the student uses commas instead of full stops (for example, in the second paragraph).

Formal letters: how to improve your response

- Use the correct layout (see pages 108–109).
- Plan what you want to say before you start.
- In your first paragraph explain exactly what you are writing about.
- Have a clear viewpoint.
- Always be polite in the way you write. Being rude and abrupt will not get you high marks.
- Take care with your spelling especially of simple words.
- Check you have not used a comma when you need a full stop.
- Remember that if you start a letter 'Dear Sir' or 'Dear Madam' you need to finish it with 'Yours faithfully'.
- If you start a letter with 'Dear Mr …' or 'Dear Mrs …' you should end it with 'Yours sincerely'.
- You may be asked to write to a newspaper. If you are, remember that your letter will begin 'Dear Sir/Madam' and the title above the address you are writing to should be 'The Editor'.

Putting it into practice

Discuss with a classmate what you have learned in this section. Think about:

- the way in which a formal letter is set out and organised
- how it is different from an informal letter (think about the style you should use)
- what you need to do to gain a high mark (think about planning and accuracy)
- the different approaches you could take if writing a letter on a different task. Plan out what you could write about:
  - banning smoking in public places
  - raising the driving age
  - any other topic you feel strongly about.

In the future:

- learn and use the features of a formal letter
- always proof-read your letters for sentence structure, punctuation and spelling. Make sure you know how to use and spell 'Yours sincerely' and 'Yours faithfully'.

Your learning

This lesson will help you to:

- practise an exam task on a formal letter
- develop a secure approach to writing a formal letter.

When writing a formal letter remember to use the correct format, opening and closure (see pages 108–109). Use a polite tone and plan your content.

Activity 1

Write your own formal letter in response to the exam task below.

A television magazine (*What's on TV* for example) has invited readers to give their views on the standard of programmes on television. The magazine is offering a cash prize for the best response. Write your letter. [20]

You may like to think about the following in your answer:

- *programmes you enjoy*
- *programmes that you feel are less interesting*
- *programmes about things you would like to see.*

Examiner tips

- Plan out what you are going to write using the bullet points.
- Think carefully about your opening paragraph.
- Include references to some television programmes. Don't just write in a general way.
- Remember why you are writing – to give your views on the programmes.

Peer/Self-assessment activity

Check your answer to Activity I. Use the mark scheme on pages 106 and 107.

- Have you included your address and date?
- Have you included the recipient's address?
- Is your salutation correct?
- Does the opening paragraph introduce the topic?
- How well do the middle paragraphs make points clearly and effectively?
- Is the concluding paragraph effective?
- Is the closure of your letter correct?
- Is your letter long enough (one and a half to two sides)?
- Have you checked your letter for errors and corrected them? (Think particularly about the commas and full stops.)
- How could you improve your letter?

Reports

What do you need to know about reports?

- **Audience:** often to a person you don't know, or know in a more formal way. It could be your local council, head teacher, school council.
- **Purpose:** to inform, advise or persuade. Provides information to those who can act on it, for example about the provision of public transport in an area.
- **Language:** formal.
- **Tone:** respectful, not rude. Put your views strongly with clear points. Support them with evidence.

If you write a report in the exam, you will:

- be told who the report is for
- be told what it is about
- need to lay out your report as shown opposite
- need to plan and organise your report as shown.

Activity 1

Read the report and comments opposite. These show you the features of a report. The student was asked to write a report for the headteacher and governors of a school about the possibility of creating a Year II common room.

1 Try writing your own report. Read the task below, set for the exam.

> **Your Community Council is organising a fun run. It has asked you to recommend three charities that could benefit from the money made. Write your report and in the conclusion give your personal opinion about the most worthy cause. [20]**
>
> *In your report you may like to include:*
>
> - *details of the three charities*
> - *why each charity is worthy of support*
> - *your opinion, with reasons, on which charity should be chosen*
> - *any other aspect you feel is important.*

2 Plan the report you will write. It needs to be one and a half to two sides long. Use the report opposite and the notes below to help you.

- **Introduction:** make it clear who you are, who you are writing the report for and what it is about.
- **Numbered paragraphs:** cover each of the bullet points in the task. You could use each bullet point to help create your numbered headings. Decide what will go under each one.
- **Include enough detail:** if your answer is short you will lose marks.
- **Concluding paragraph:** say what you think should happen next – perhaps a meeting to discuss the issue.

3 Now write your report. Use your plan to help you. Use the format shown opposite.

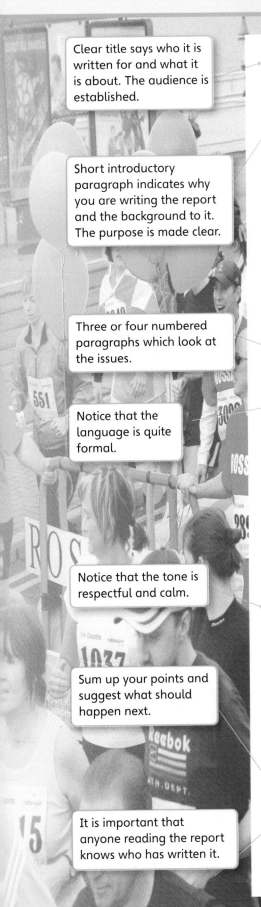

Clear title says who it is written for and what it is about. The audience is established.

Short introductory paragraph indicates why you are writing the report and the background to it. The purpose is made clear.

Three or four numbered paragraphs which look at the issues.

Notice that the language is quite formal.

Notice that the tone is respectful and calm.

Sum up your points and suggest what should happen next.

It is important that anyone reading the report knows who has written it.

A report to the head teacher and governors about the possibility of creating a Year 11 common room

Introduction

Year 11 school council members were asked by the head teacher to prepare a report on using unused rooms in the main school building as a Year 11 common room. As a member of the Year 11 council, I have talked to other Year 11 students and these are our findings.

1. Background

As you know, the school has a number of rooms that are no longer used. We believe that it would be a good idea to use these rooms as a base for the Year 11 students.

2. The benefits of having a Year 11 common room

Teachers often complain when they see Year 11 students hanging around the corridors during lunch and breaktime. A Year 11 common room could be a place where students can gather to socialise and work. It would have two clear benefits for the school. Firstly the corridors would be less crowded and it would be easier for teachers and lunchtime supervisors to keep control and secondly, the students would be given an opportunity to revise and complete homework.

3. Where the common room could be positioned

The three rooms numbered 18, 19 and 20 have not been used for teaching for some time and are conveniently situated towards the end of the school building. We propose that these rooms could be used for different purposes: Room 18 could be a social area with coffee making facilities and easy chairs; Room 19, which would be a 'quiet' room, could be used for study and revision; and Room 20 could be kitted out as a games room.

4. When the students could use the common room

Obviously these rooms could only be used before school, at breaktimes, lunchtimes and after school. We propose that a group of trusted Year 11 student keyholders be given the responsibility of opening and locking the rooms at the appropriate times.

5. Keeping order in the rooms

We know that you will be worried about the discipline in these rooms and so we are proposing that a group of students is responsible for making sure that the privilege is not misused. We think that there will need to be rules …

Conclusion

We hope that you are persuaded that creating a Year 11 common room would be a good idea and we look forward to meeting with you to discuss the proposal in more detail.

Mary Brown

(Secretary to the Year 11 Council)

Here is a student response to the exam task below. Read the answer and the examiner comments.
Your Community Council is organising a fun run. It has asked you to recommend three charities
which could benefit from the money made. Write your report and in the conclusion give your
personal opinion about the most worthy cause. [20]

Extract typical of a E grade answer

Student 1

This is my report to the comunity council about the fun run charity appeal.

There are three charities we could support, they are Cancer appeal, NSPCC and RSPCA.

These are my thoughts on these charities, the cancer one is good because a lot of people die of cancer and my mates aunt died two years ago from it. I think that this is a good one to choose.

The NSPCC looks after kids who are in trouble and I think that it deserves to be supported because lots of kids get abused by there parents and we should try to stop that happening.

The RSPCA looks after animals and none of us likes to see animals hurt by creul people, they can't answer back or look after themselves and they should be looked after properly and given food and not kicked around or hurt.

I think the cancer one is best and we should give our money to that one when people have done the run.

Yours sincerly

Gemma Green

Content and organisation

Strong point

- There is a clear sense of purpose and a good understanding of what each charity does.

Weak points

- An incorrect format has been used. The ending is suitable for a letter but not a report.
- The student could have used sub-headings.
- The tone and style are too informal for a report (for example, 'My mates aunt...', 'kids').
- The work seems to be rushed with not enough care taken to develop the points (for example, the last paragraph).
- The report is too short.

Sentence structure, punctuation and spelling

Strong points

- Much of the spelling is accurate.
- Some of the punctuation is accurate.

Weak points

- Phrases are repeated ('There are...' and 'looks after...').
- Commas are used instead of full stops, for example in the second paragraph.
- The following words were misspelled by the student: 'community' 'cruel', sincerely'.
- The student missed some apostrophes ('Mate's').

Peer/Self-assessment activity

1 Read the report written in an exam and the examiner comments.

2 Can you note down at least one strong point and one thing to improve in your report for each heading below:
   - content
   - organisation
   - sentence structure
   - punctuation
   - spelling?

Reports: how to improve your response

- Read the question carefully. Think about what you are being asked to do.
- Plan your report. Make quick notes on what kind of content you need.
- Organise your points into a sensible structure before you begin to write.
- Remember you need an introduction, three or four numbered points and a conclusion.

- Think about your audience. What do they already know? What do they need to know?
- Write with a formal rather than a 'chatty' style.
- Take great care with your spelling and punctuation.
- When you have finished, check your work carefully and look at your commas in particular. Ask yourself the question: 'Do I need a comma here or a full stop?'
- Do not be afraid to make corrections.

Putting it into practice

In the future:
- learn and use the features of a report
- think about the audience carefully
- always check your report for sentence structure, punctuation and spelling.

Your learning

This lesson will help you to:

- practise using key features of a report
- develop a secure approach to writing a report.

When you are writing a report, remember you need a formal tone and numbered points so the report is easy to read. Plan carefully before you start.

Activity 1

Write a report in response to the exam task below.

Your town or community council are worried about the problem of young people hanging around in the streets at night. The council has asked students in your school or college to suggest ways in which the facilities for young people in the area could be improved.

You have been asked to write a report on the facilities and make recommendations for new facilities. [20]

In your report you may like to think about:

- *the reasons why young people are hanging round on the streets*

- *the existing facilities*

- *the new facilities that could be created to provide young people with something to do*

- *any other issues that you feel relevant.*

Examiner tips

If you use statistics in your report make sure they are sensible and realistic.

1 Check your answer to Activity 1. Use the mark scheme on pages 106 and 107.

- Did you set out your report properly with a title, introduction, numbered points and a conclusion?
- Did you think about:
  who you were writing the report for
  what they already knew
  what they needed to know?
- Were you careful with the language you used and did you keep the report formal?
- Did you write a report that will be useful to the person or people it is written for? Did you include points that were likely to change their view?
- Did you put in enough detail? Remember, if your report is not long enough (about one and a half to two sides), you will not get a high mark.
- Did you check your work to get rid of any careless errors? Did you think carefully about your use of commas and full stops?
- How could you improve your report?

Your learning

This lesson will help you to:

- understand the features of an article
- write an interesting article.

What do you need to know about articles?

- **Audience:** Usually teenage magazine readers but could be for older or younger readers.
- **Purpose:** to give information, advice or put forward an opinion.
- **Language:** less formal that a report. Usually quite 'chatty' but this will depend on the audience and topic.
- **Tone:** This will depend on the, task but usually not very serious.

If you write an article in the exam, you will:

- be told who the article is for
- be told what it is about
- need to lay out your article as shown below
- need to plan and organise your article as shown opposite.

Activity 1

Read the article and comments opposite. These show you the features of an article. The student was asked to write an article for a teenage magazine about a favourite sport or pastime, trying to persuade others to take part in it.

1 Try writing your own article. Read the task below, taken from the exam.

> **Write a lively article for a local newspaper on what it is like to be a teenager in the 21st century. [20]**
>
> *You may like to think about:*
>
> - *relationships with your parents*
> - *relationships with your friends*
> - *the problems teenagers have*
> - *changing from being seen as a child to being seen as an adult.*

2 Plan the article you will write. It needs to be one and a half to two pages long. Use the article opposite and think about the following.

- What exactly is the task asking you to do?
- Think carefully about the word 'lively'. This word gives you a clue as to the tone and style you should aim for.
- You could use the bullet points as sub-headings but do not be afraid of thinking of better ones.
- Plan your work before you begin to write.
- Think about your audience, which could be people your own age as well as older people.
- Make the article personal – use evidence from your own life and experiences or those of people you know.
- Remember to check your work for mistakes when you have finished.

3 Now write your article. Use your plan to help you. Use the format shown opposite.

Good catchy title – designed to attract readers

Begins with a question – makes the reader think

Reference to 'old ones' creates a link with the intended audience (teenagers)

Clear introductory paragraph – introduces the subject

You can use sub-headings if you want to

Aware of task – to persuade

Article looks at the discipline needed – it doesn't just stress the fun element

Stress on the positives too

Clear conclusion summing the article up

Fabulous Football

Do like to keep active? If you do, football is the game for you. We are told all the time by the old ones that we are a fat and lazy generation. Football is one way to prove them wrong. Playing football brings all sorts of benefits.

Like to be with your friends?

There's nothing like football for helping you to make and keep friends. You meet with a particular purpose and train hard to win matches. This gives the players a good sense of belonging. Football can also give you a very good social life. You are never short of company if you want to go out at night.

Dedication

It requires dedication though. If you aren't prepared to attend practices regularly and take orders and advice from the manager and trainer then it's not the game for you. There's no 'I' in the word 'team'. You are not a popular or good team member if you are never prepared to pass the ball so that some else can score. It's not a game where you go for personal glory. If you want that go and play snooker or darts.

Competition

Competition is good for you. It sharpens up your reflexes and gives you a purpose in life. Wanting to win is not a bad thing as long as you don't break the rules to do it. There's nothing like the feeling you get before a big match when all the team are united in determination to thrash the opponents. That really gets the adrenalin rushing and it's much healthier than sitting in front of a game station.

Take my advice. If you want to stay fit and active, have friends, get a bit of excitement into your life and feel as if you have accomplished something, join a football team. You won't regret it.

Examiner tips

You won't carry on reading an article if you aren't interested by the first paragraph. If you want people to read yours, you must make the reader want to read on. The first paragraph must do this.

GradeStudio

On pages 122–125 are two student responses to the exam task below. Read the answers and the examiner comments.

Write a lively article for a local newspaper on what it is like to be a teenager in the 21st century. [20]

Student 1

Does life improve when your a teenager?

When you become a teenager it is hard as everybodys hormones are all over the place, you tend to loose friends and gain friends, but that is life.

In your teenage years you gain a lot of funny memries with your friends and you go into relationships that sometimes that you regret and sometimes you dont, all this helps you to grow up and find out who you are if you like the real you.

For me becoming a teenager was hard as i lived with my mum and step father and on my 13th birthday i just wanted my real dad there. things got better over the years and your friends help you

Examiner comments

Content and organisation

Strong points

- The article has a title, but could also have included the writer's name.
- Some good points about being a teenager are made.
- The student does refer to personal experience. They are honest in the way they do this.
- There is some sense of audience.

Weak points

- The article is far too short. The student has not developed her points. This reduces the mark.
- Sub-headings would have made the article more interesting.
- The student only refers to their own experiences. They would have done better if they had thought about other teenagers as well.
- The bullet points have not been used to help shape the article.
- The article is not very 'lively'.

Sentence structure, punctuation and spelling

Strong points

- The article is laid out in paragraphs.
- Most spellings are correct.
- Some punctuation is accurate.

Weak points

- The following words were misspelled by the student: 'lose', 'memries'.
- The student missed apostrophes: for example, 'everybody's', 'don't'.
- Commas are used instead of full stops (for example, in the first paragraph).
- Full stops are missed out (for example, at the end of the article).
- The student uses 'i' when they should use 'I'.

Articles: how to improve your response

- Think about the task before you start to write. Decide in your mind exactly what you are being asked to do.
- Plan your article before you begin.
- Think of an interesting title. Use sub-headings if you want to.
- Remember who you are writing for. If it is a teenage audience, remember that they will know a lot of the things you know. If the article is for an adult audience you may need to explain things more carefully.
- Try to make it lively and interesting. For example, you can use humour if the task is not a serious one.
- Take special care with the way you begin and end your article. At the beginning you need to 'catch' your audience with something interesting and at the end you want to lave the reader thinking that he or she has read something enjoyable.
- Remember, if you write too short an article, you will lose marks.
- When you have finished, check your work to make sure you have not made mistakes with commas and apostrophes and the spelling of simple words.

Putting it into practice

In the future:

- plan your article before you write
- think about your audience carefully
- always check your article for sentence structure, punctuation and spelling.

Tantrums, Texting and Teens

Being a teen is the best time in a persons life. Or is it? Chloe Baker finds out.

I am now 15 years old and am half way through my teenage years. It's safe to say I kinda like it.

I'm now given a say in what time I go to bed, usually 11 o'clock, and I can go out wearing what I want, within reason. Obviously no leather micro skirts and see through crop tops with a face full of make up. I'm not that free! I can also go to places further away with my mates without my parents having to take me. I got the train all the way to Manchester last week!

I get on better with my Mum and Dad too now I am a bit older. When I was a young teen I argued with my Mum a lot and we had lots of rows about who I was supposed to be friends with and where I could go. Mum didn't like the clothes I wanted to buy either and it was always a struggle to beg enough money to keep up with my friend's fashion hints. I remember Dad always kept away from these arguments. It would have been nice if he had backed me up but I suppose he wanted to keep in Mum's good books. Things are much better now though because Mum and I have come to an understanding about what I am able to do and what I'm not and now she is much more like an elder sister. I realise now that she was only worried about me.

Although all the things I've written make being a teen sound great, there is a downside. There always is, isn't there?

I'm given more responsibility which can be great when going out but I'm talking about a different kind of responsibility. For example, all the controlled assessment and homework you are given. It is your responsibility to get it done and as you get older, you gradually get more and more. I struggle to keep up. Of course it doesn't help with your parents nagging you all the time. I hate it when they do but try not to be too harsh on them; they are only trying to help.

Anyway I think I must leave you as Mum is saying I should get on with some work. I've got some streets to wander too! Being a teen is not half as bad as some make it out to be!

Examiner comments

Content and organisation

Strong points

- There is a good understanding of the purpose of the article.
- The title is interesting.
- The short opening paragraph introduces the subject matter.
- The student has made good use of the bullet points.
- The article is balanced. The student looks at the good things about being a teenager and then at the less attractive aspects.
- The content is presented in a lively way (for example, 'Obviously no leather micro skirts and see through "crop tops"').
- The student uses her own personal experience.
- The tone is friendly and warm (for example, 'I'm not that free!').
- There is a good sense of audience (for example, the opening and closing paragraphs).

Weak points

- The student could have referred to other teenagers' experience as well as her own.
- The first sentence of the final paragraph is more suited to a letter than an article.
- The range of aspects the student discusses is rather limited.

Sentence structure, punctuation and spelling

Strong points

- The student makes no spelling errors.
- Punctuation is accurate apart from the missed apostrophe in 'persons'.

- **Weak points**
- The student begins a number of sentences in the same way, for example, 'I...'.

Peer/Self-assessment activity

1 Read the two articles written in an exam and the examiner comments. Which response is your article closest to? Why?

2 Can you note down at least one strong point and one thing to improve in your article for each heading below:
- content
- organisation
- sentence structure
- punctuation
- spelling?

Your learning

This lesson will help you to:

- practise using key features of an article
- develop a secure approach to writing an article.

When writing an article:

- be as interesting as you can be
- think carefully about who you are writing it for – your audience
- plan before you start
- use bullet points if provided
- take care that your tone and style is suitable for the audience
- write one to two sides
- check your work.

Activity 1

Now write your own article, in response to the exam task below.

Write an article for a primary school newsletter in which you tell the Year 6 class what life is like in your secondary school. [20]

You may like to think about the following:

- *a friendly introduction*
- *how your school is different from the primary school*
- *the subjects you do*
- *some advice about moving up to your secondary school*
- *a friendly conclusion.*

When you are attempting this task, think about all the things you have learned about writing an article in this section of the book. In particular:

- think about your audience – here it is Year 6 pupils
- think about the tone and style you will need to use for younger readers
- think about what will be worrying them and the kind of information they will need
- use your own experience in your article
- remember to be interesting – younger children will not read things that bore them.
- check your work.

Examiner tips

In tasks such as these, be honest and draw on your personal experience and observations.

Peer/Self-assessment activity

Check your answer to Activity I. Use the mark scheme on pages I06 and I07.

- Did you have an interesting title?
- Is the article set out in paragraphs with subheadings?
- Is the first paragraph likely to interest I0-year-olds?
- Have you followed the bullet points to give your article some shape?
- Did you use your own experience to help to explain your ideas?
- Did you finish your article with a pleasant and reassuring final paragraph?
- Would primary school pupils enjoy reading your article or would they be bored?
- Are your spelling and punctuation accurate?
- How could you improve your article?

2.5 Leaflets

Your learning

This lesson will help you to:

- understand the features of leaflets
- write an effective leaflet.

What do you need to know about leaflets?

- **Purpose:** to inform, advise, persuade. They tell people things they need to know, for example about health issues, such as the risks of smoking, or about places to visit, such as theme parks or holiday locations.
- **Audience:** most would aim for the widest audience (for example, smoking, holidays); some aim for young people (for example, paint-balling); some for older people (for example, old age pensions).
- **Language:** needs to match purpose and audience. For example, for young people the language could be informal, while a leaflet about a health issue will be serious in nature.
- **Tone:** needs to match the purpose and audience. For example, a leaflet advertising a holiday attraction will be exciting, while a leaflet about the dangers of fire would be formal.

If you write a leaflet in the exam, you will:

- be told who the leaflet is for
- be told what it is about
- need to lay out your leaflet as shown opposite
- need to plan and organise your leaflet as shown opposite.

Activity 1

Read the leaflet and comments opposite. These show you the features of a leaflet. The leaflet was written to give information and advice about what children should know about fire.

Read the task below, set for the exam.

> **Your local sports complex is not getting enough people through the doors. Write a leaflet explaining the benefits of good health and persuading more people to use the complex. [20]**

In your answer you may like to think about the following:

- *an interesting title*
- *why it is sensible to have a healthy lifestyle*
- *the facilities available in the sports complex*
- *any other details readers would find useful.*

1 Plan the leaflet you will write. It needs to be one and a half to two sides long. Use the leaflet opposite to help you.

2 Now write your leaflet. Use your plan to help you. Use the format shown opposite.

Immediate appeal to the audience (parents) who will read the leaflet because they want to keep their children safe

Paragraphs are short and clear

Instructions are simple and direct – the audience is kept in mind

Clear title so that anybody reading it will know what it is about straight away – the purpose is clear

What your children should know about fire

You will want to make sure children are always safe. This includes teaching them how to prevent a fire and what to do in the advent of one.

You will probably need to talk about fire safety with children more than once, to make sure that they have remembered and understood what you have taught them.

As a general rule younger children, around five and below, should be given clear instructions about what they should and shouldn't do. With older children, it's better to explain why.

The content explains carefully why parents should behave in a certain way – again this is strongly aware of the audience

It's important that they know how to prevent a fire:

- Not to touch or play with matches, lighters, candles, electrical appliances or sockets.
- To tell a grown up if they see matches or lighters lying around.
- To be extra careful near fires and heaters.
- Never to switch on the cooker.
- Not to touch saucepans.
- Not to put things on top of heaters or lights.

Bullet points are used for the advice

Top tip

Share these safety messages with your children so they know what to do in the event of a fire.

Tell them:

- If you see smoke or flames tell a grown-up straight away.
- Get out of the building as quickly as you can if there is a fire.
- Don't go back for anything, even toys or pets.
- Find a phone. (You might need to go to the neighbours to find one.)
- Call 999. Ask for Fire and Rescue Service and tell them your address. (You might want to practise making this call with your children and you will need to make sure they know their address.)

- Only call 999 in a real emergency.
- Never hide if there is a fire. Get out as quickly as you can.
- If there's smoke, crawl along the floor (the air will be clearer down there).
- Go into a room with a window if the way out is blocked.
- Put bedding or towels along the bottom of the door to stop smoke getting in.
- Open the window and call 'HELP FIRE'.

GET OUT STAY OUT AND CALL 999

Sub-heading used to divide the leaflet up

The language is simple and easy to understand

Illustration to make the leaflet more attractive. If you want to show illustrations in your leaflet simply draw a box and write in it what the picture will be.

Here is a student response to the exam task below. Read the answer and the examiner comments.

Your local sports complex is not getting enough people through the doors. Write a leaflet explaining the benefits of good health and persuading more people to use the complex. [20]

Student 1

Do you need to get fit?

Put too much weight on lately?

Worried about not keeping up with the children?

What you need is a few sessions in our Fitness complex.

What you can do

Weight training

Treadmill work

Learn yoga

Do step classes

Learn to dance the salsa

Swim

Have the help of a personal trainer

All you need to do is to join our fitness club to see all the benefits.

You'll soon be a fitter slimmer person

For details contact www.keepfitfacilities.com

Typical E grade answer

Examiner comments

Sentence structures, punctuation and spelling

Strong points

- The spelling is accurate.
- Most of the punctuation is correct apart from a couple of missing full stops.

Weak points

- So much of the answer is taken up with lists that there are not enough sentences to show the student's ability to write fluently.

Content and organisation

Strong points

* The title is interesting. Using questions helps to lead into the leaflet.
* There is some coverage of the range of activities in the complex.
* The sense of audience is good. The student knows who they need to attract to the centre.
* The sense of purpose is clear.

Weak points

* The work is too short.
* The student uses lists, which means that the examiner does not have many full sentences to mark. This reduces the mark.
* The format could be better.

Peer/Self-assessment activity

1 Read the leaflet written in an exam and the examiner comments

2 Can you note down at least one strong point and one thing to improve in your leaflet for each heading below:
  * content
  * organisation
  * sentence structure
  * punctuation
  * spelling?

Leaflets: how to improve your response

To improve your response you need to do the following.

* Think carefully about what you are being asked to do.
* Think carefully about whom you are writing the leaflet for. It may be for older people, young people or for all ages. You must remember this when you are choosing your details.
* Remember to match your tone to the purpose. If you are writing a leaflet on a serious issue, you need to be formal in the way you write. If it is not so serious you can use a more 'chatty' style.
* Set your leaflet out with sub-headings and sections. This will help the reader find his or her way around it.
* Use your own experience if you can.
* Make sure that you write in full sentence and do not list.
* Check your work when you have finished. Make sure you have not used a comma when you need a full stop and check that your apostrophes are correct.

Putting it into practice

This task asks you to write a persuasive leaflet. Remember that some tasks you may be given in the examination may ask you to write informational leaflets.

* Think of a place that you like visiting and that you think people of your age would also enjoy.
* Plan a leaflet intended to persuade young people to go there.
* Think of a main heading and sub-headings.
* Think carefully about how you will persuade the reader to go.
* Write your leaflet and remember to check it when you have finished for spelling and punctuation errors.
* Remember that you do not need to use illustrations but you can indicate where they may be placed if you want to.
* Ask a fellow student to look at your plan and to give an opinion.

Your learning

This lesson will help you to:

- practise using key features of a leaflet
- develop a secure approach to writing a leaflet.

When writing a leaflet:

- get a clear picture of your audience in your mind before you start
- think about what you are being asked to do in the leaflet. It could be to persuade, advise or inform; it may be to do all three
- use a good title and sub-headings
- use a style and tone suitable for the audience and purpose
- remember not to list things; instead write in full sentences
- check your work when you have finished.

Activity 1

Now write your own leaflet in response to the exam task below.

Write a leaflet for parents with small children explaining the dangers of the Internet and giving some advice on how they can be avoided. [20]

In your leaflet you may like to think about:

- *a suitable title*
- *the different aspects of Internet that may be a danger for children*
- *the advice you would give to parents to keep children safe*
- *a suitable conclusion*
- *any other aspects that you think are important.*

Examiner tips

Put into practice all the things you have learned in this section and be particularly careful with the audience (parents) and the purpose (to inform and advise). Remind yourself of the important things to remember about this type of writing by re-reading the 'When writing a leaflet' section at the top of this page.

Peer/Self-assessment activity

I Check your answer to Activity I. Use the mark scheme on pages I06 and I07.

- Did you have a good interesting title?
- Did you use sub-headings to make your leaflet look appealing and to guide the reader to the different sections?
- Did keep in mind the fact that your audience was parents?
- Did you use language that was suitable for this audience?
- Did you think carefully about the dangers and explain them to the audience?
- Did you follow up the part about the dangers with advice on how to help the children avoid them?
- Was your advice clear?
- Did you write enough (one and half to two sides)?
- Did you end your leaflet with a suitable conclusion?
- Did you check your work for errors in punctuation and spelling?
- How could you improve your letter?

Your learning

This lesson will help you to:

- explore what makes a good speech
- learn how to construct a speech.

In the examination, you may be asked to write a talk. This is the same as a speech.

What do you need to know about writing a speech?

- **Audience:** often students in your school but it could be more general if, for example, you were writing a speech for a radio phone-in show.
- **Purpose:** to inform or persuade. This will depend on your task.
- **Language:** this will depend on your audience. A speech to children, for example, would have to be fairly simple.
- **Tone:** generally formal rather than chatty but this will again depend on your audience.

If you write a speech in the exam, you will:

- be told who it is for
- be told what it is about
- need to lay out your speech as shown opposite
- need to plan and organise your speech as shown opposite.

Examiner tips

Your speech will be better if you think carefully about your audience and shape what you say to suit it.

Activity 1

Read the speech and comments opposite. These show you the features of a speech. The student was asked to write a speech about whether or not teenagers have an easy life. The speech was for students in the class.

1 Try writing your own speech. Read the task below, set for the exam.

> **You have been asked to make a speech to junior school pupils starting secondary school. [20]**
>
> *Think about the following when writing your speech:*
>
> - *introducing yourself*
> - *introducing your secondary school*
> - *aspects that they will find different in moving to secondary school*
> - *things that the younger children will be worried about*
> - *a suitable conclusion.*

2 Plan the speech you will write. It needs to be one and a half to two sides long. Use the speech opposite and the notes below to help you.

- **Open with a welcome/greeting to your audience. This will be brief and simple – 'Good morning Year 6. My name is Jake.'**
- **Outline the subject of the speech: 'I'm here to talk to you about moving to secondary school.'**
- **Make three or four key points. Base these on the bullet points in the task. Remember your audience. It is a good idea to number your points.**
- **Write a conclusion that is reassuring for the pupils.**
- **End by thanking them for listening and wishing them well in the future.**

Clear opening statement so your audience knows what you are talking about

Shows awareness of audience

Use of rhetorical questions to involve the audience

Again shows awareness of audience; also note use of emotive language ('nagged')

The student begins to make an argument about the stresses of teenage life

Another rhetorical question to keep the audience interested

In a speech you need paragraphs but you don't need sub-headings

Personal experience to support the argument

Moves to the second part of the argument about parental pressure

Exaggeration used

Sees and states the other side of the argument about parents

Concluding paragraph summing up the arguments again showing awareness of audience

Finishes the speech with thanks

Today I am here to discuss whether teenagers have an easy life. Many people think that teenagers in the 21st century have such easy lives, but this is not all true. We teens are constantly criticised by the media for being violent and drunk thugs in hoodies. We aren't all like that! Don't you agree that teenagers lives can be very hectic with controlled assessment and exams, getting the right group of friends and dealing with peer pressure? Besides that we constantly have to worry about being nagged by our parents!

We teenagers are always taking some sort of exam in school. Sometimes they are just little exams in the classroom and other times they are our GCSEs, our most important exams as everyone keeps saying. Aren't our lives hectic enough, with GCSEs and all the different pieces of controlled assessment we have to write without the constant nagging from parents and teachers about getting good results? It's a wonder it doesn't drive us insane.

Because of all the school work and different activities that we teenagers do in and out of school, our lives can be very stressful. In the end we get tired just thinking about all the work we have to do. I have to fit in all the loads of homework our teachers keep giving us and do a part-time job at the weekend so I have some money. It would be nice to have a bit of time for a social life too!

Teenagers have so much schoolwork to do that we barely have any spare time, but when we do we like to have our freedom. When we do go out, our parents want to know where we are going, with whom and when we will be back. Isn't that really annoying? It makes me want to scream! Our parents don't need to know where we are every minute of the day. I understand that our parents are only trying to look after us but we are not children and we can fend for ourselves. Sometimes we just need to get away from their nagging but they put us under more pressure phoning us and asking where we are.

To finish off, I hope I have convinced you that teenagers have hectic and stressful lives. We get too much schoolwork to do and not enough time to enjoy ourselves. We know what it is like to be a teenager. Lots of adults have forgotten how hard it is and only want to criticise us. Thank you for listening. I am sure you'll agree with what I have said.

3 Now write your speech. Use your plan to help you. Use the format shown above.

Remember, when you are writing a speech, you need to hold the attention of the people listening.

Here is a student response to the exam task below. Read the answer and the examiner comments.

You have been asked to make a speech to junior school pupils starting secondary school. [20]

Extract typical of a C grade answer

Student 1

Hello. My name is Dean and I've come to tell you all about what the life of a pupil is like in the High School. I rember how I felt when I was your age. Lots of people told me horrible stories about what would happen to me but what I want to say is that none of those things happened to me or anyone I know so stop worrying!

One of my main worries when I came up was the fear of getting lost. The High School is really big compared with your primary school but you'll soon get used to it. When you arrive some students will show you around and you'll have maps of the school in your planners. The teachers and older students will be happy to help you. As I say, you'll get a planner. We all have a planner. It is a book where you note down your homeworks and other things.

That brings me to my next point- homework! Don't worry, You wont get much at the start of the year. I rember that the first week we just had to cover our books and that wasn't very hard! You will get more as you go up the school but as long as you do it the day you are given it youll be OK. When you get up to Years 10 and 11 youll get controlled assessment tasks to do but you needn't worry about that yet. If you can't do your homework, ask the teacher to explain it again. They are quite willing to help.

One of the things you'll find different is the fact that you have to move around the school a lot. You'll soon get used to this so don't worry if you are bit late for your lessons in the first week or so. The teachers wont eat you! But I wouldn't make a habit of it. They do get a bit cross if you are late and have no excuse. Generaly the teachers are kind though and you'll get along very well as long as you behave and don't mess them about.

Are you worried about making friends? Well, don't be. Generaly they put at least a couple of people from the same junior school in a registration class and so you will know some one. You'll quickly make new friends especially if you join one of the clubs. There are lots of these and your form teacher will tell you all about them.

So I hope you can see that there is no need to get uptight about coming up to the High School. It will be a challenge for you but I am sure you'll all do well. Thanks for listening to me and good luck at the big school.

Examiner comments

Content and organisation
Strong points
- The speech is a good length.
- The writer introduces himself clearly.
- The sense of audience is strong. For example, 'I rem(em)ber how I felt when I was your age…'. The writer has thought about what worried him when he went up to the High School.
- The purpose of the speech is clear. The student reassures the young pupils (for example, 'Don't worry…').
- The language and vocabulary choices are well suited to the 10- to 11-year-old audience (for example, 'You'll soon get used to this…').
- The tone is friendly and pleasant.
- The writer sensibly makes use of his own experiences.
- The writer has made the task real to himself.
- The writer uses repetition (for example, '… you'll get a planner. We all have a planner…').
- The student uses rhetorical questions (for example, 'Are you worried about making friends?').
- The writer ends with thanks to the audience.

Weak points
None.

Sentence structure, punctuation and spelling
Strong points
- Virtually all the spelling is accurate.
- Punctuation is mostly correct.
- There is a variety of sentence structures.

Weak points
- The following words were misspelled by the student: 'remember' and 'generally'.
- The student missed some apostrophes: 'won't', 'you'll'.

Speeches: how to improve your response
- If you are allowed to choose your own topic, talk about something that is of interest to you but remember that your audience may not know anything about it so be careful you don't use words they will not understand.
- Before starting to write, plan what you intend to say.

Peer/Self-assessment activity

Can you note down at least one strong point and one thing to improve in your speech for each heading below:
- content
- organisation
- sentence structure
- punctuation
- spelling?

Your learning

This lesson will help you to:

- practise using key features of writing a speech
- develop a secure approach to writing a speech.

When writing a speech, remember:

- Think about your task. What exactly is it asking you to do (the purpose)?
- Think about the audience. You need to shape your language and tone to the audience.
- Remember to introduce yourself and write a suitable conclusion.
- Think in terms of three or four main points you want to make (the bullet points will help you here).
- Most of all, think yourself into the task. If it is not real for you, then you will not write well or convincingly.
- Always check your work for spelling and punctuation errors.

Activity 1

Now write your own speech, in response to the exam task below.

There is a discussion on a radio late night phone-in programme about a proposal to raise the legal age for the sale of alcohol to 21 to stop teenage binge drinking. Write the speech you would make on this topic. [20]

You may like to think about the following points in your speech:

- *introducing yourself*
- *your own thoughts about the problem of binge drinking*
- *any arguments for raising the legal age for the sale of alcohol to 21*
- *any arguments against it*
- *your conclusion in which you state your own views on whether the age should be changed.*

Examiner tips

In this task you have to construct an argument.

- It will be helpful if you plan before you start it.
- Note down the arguments for changing or not changing the age as you see it.
- You may like simply to look at one side of the argument but your work will probably be better if you look at both sides of the issue.
- Do not forget to make your own view clear in your conclusion.
- Remember your audience is general.
- Some people are likely to feel strongly about this topic. Take care with the way you express yourself. Be polite, don't be rude or abrupt.
- Keep in mind all the things you have learned in this section about writing a speech.

Peer/Self-assessment activity

Check your answer to Activity I. Use the mark scheme on pages I06 and I07.

- Did you introduce yourself?
- Did you make it clear what you were talking about in your introduction?
- Did you paragraph your work making use of the bullet points?
- Did you make clear points about your views on the legal age to buy alcohol?
- Did you conclude the speech with a clear statement of your view?
- Did you write enough? Short answers will not achieve high marks.
- Did you think about your audience?
- Did you make your speech interesting and personal?
- Did you check your work to get rid of those obvious errors?
- How could you improve your speech?

Your learning

This lesson will help you to:

- learn about writing reviews, in particular of books, films and music.

What do you need to know about writing a review?

- **Audience:** generally a teenage magazine.
- **Purpose:** to be able to give your opinion on a book, film, TV programme or CD.
- **Language:** informal.
- **Tone:** lively and entertaining.

If you write a review in the exam, you will:

- be told who it is for – the audience
- be given a choice about what you review
- need to lay out your review as shown opposite
- need to plan and organise your review as shown opposite.

Activity 1

Read the task below, set for the exam.

Write a review suitable for a teenage magazine of a book, film, television programme or CD. [20]

In your review you may like to think about the following:

- *an introduction giving the reader some of the details the book, film, television programme or CD you are reviewing*
- *things you liked about the book, film, television programme or CD*
- *aspect you were less impressed with*
- *a conclusion in which you give your final judgement.*

Look at the reviews written by two students, shown on pages 141 and 142, and use these to help you complete Activity 2 on page 143.

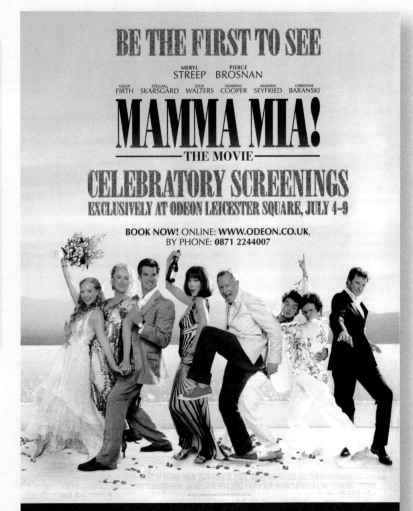

This student was given the task of writing a film review.

Clear titles used throughout the review – helps to guide the reader

Entertaining opening paragraph to interest the reader

Details of actors given

Brief summary of the film, which does not give too much of the plot away

The student looks at what is enjoyable about the film

A new paragraph for the weaknesses

Humour keeps the reader interested

The final paragraph sums up the writer's views in a lively way

Film review *Mamma Mia!*

What's it about?

First question, do you like ABBA? If the answer's 'no' stop reading now because if you don't, watching this film could be like extended root canal surgery.

Obviously you must like ABBA so carry on reading. The film *Mamma Mia!* is based on a stage musical in which 20 ABBA songs are woven into a story about a single mother, Donna, (played by Meryl Streep) on a Greek island. Her daughter (Sophie played by Amanda Seyfried) is getting married and unknown to her mother has invited the three men who could be her father to her wedding. When they arrive old emotions are aroused as she tries to work out who actually is the father of her daughter. Sophie always thought she would be able to work out who her father was but she is as confused as her mother.

What's good about it?

Well, the ABBA songs are as good as they always were and the acting is strong throughout the cast. If you like your romance set on an idyllic Greek island with a chorus of locals, a supporting cast easy on the eye and some pretty poor singing from Colin Firth and Pierce Brosnan, both possible fathers to Sophie, then you are in for a grand evening. Serious it isn't and when you watch it you have to believe that the songs are related to what's going on in the plot, which is rather hard at times. But it isn't just a vehicle for ABBA fans to get high on. The acting throughout is excellent and it's almost as if the cast actually believe the silly plot could really happen. The star of the show is Amanda Seyfried who can sing and does a smashing performance of 'Thank You for the Music' over the final credits. Well worth waiting for!

Weaknesses?

Leaving aside the fact that the plot creeks like an old door, there's not much to complain about. Did I mention Pierce Brosnan's singing?

Worth seeing?

If you like feel-good movies of the romcom kind then this is for you. If you are happier watching *Terminator 307*, let the girls go by themselves (they can dance in the aisles then without embarrassing you) and go and do something useful like changing the clutch on your car.

Star rating ****

This student was asked to write a review of a book they knew well.

Of Mice and Men by John Steinbeck

We are lucky to have this book as John Steinbeck's dog ate the original manuscript and Steinbeck had to start again and re-write the whole thing from memory. Thank goodness he did as it is moving tale of sadness and loneliness. Widely studied by students both here and in the US, it never seems to lose its power.

Set in the 1930s, it's about a pair of farm labourers who wander round California looking for work in the Great Depression. Both are outsiders. George is a sensible and sympathetic character who looks after his simple-minded friend Lennie. They have a dream of being able to settle down in their own place and 'live on the fat of the land' as Lennie puts it. While Lennie's huge strength makes him a useful worker on the ranch they arrive at early in the book, he has a major problem in controlling his strength and this leads to the terrible conclusion of the book.

Steinbeck paints a powerful picture of the loneliness of all the characters, not only Lennie and George, but all the others on the ranch ranging from the black man Crooks to the ranch owner's son's wife. Both play a major part in the final tragedy.

This book has no weaknesses. The characterisation is powerful and convincing and the story compelling. You want to know what happens next, which is always a good thing in a novel.

If you are lucky enough to read this book for your GCSE course, you will enjoy it though don't be surprised if you find it very sad indeed.

Opening paragraph introduces the book and gives the reader the main themes

This student does not use sub-headings but the paragraphs follow the bullet points

Main characters introduced

A brief plot summary, which does not give too much of the plot away, readers will be interested to know what the 'terrible conclusion' is

Other important characters mentioned but not investigated in detail

The student gives an evaluation of the novel and a recommendation

In the review, the student has given a 'snapshot' of the text and picked out the most important features

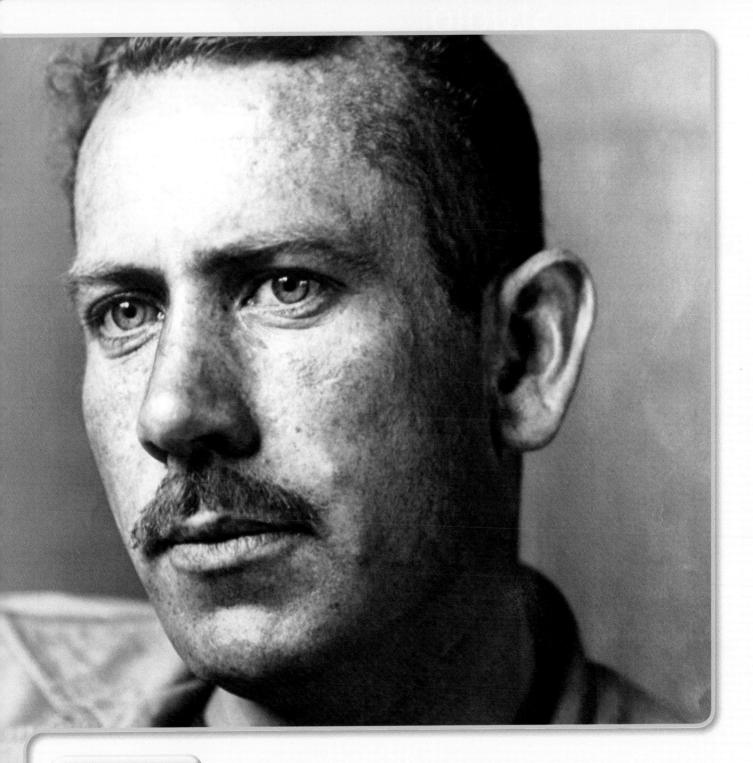

Activity 2

1   Now write your own review in response to the exam task below. Use what you have learned on these pages to help you.

    Write a review suitable for a teenage audience of a book, film, television programme or CD. [20]

2   Compare your review with the student answers on pages 144–147. Read the examiner comments. Which response is your review closest to? How could you improve?

GradeStudio

On pages 144–147 are two student responses to the exam task below. Read the answers and the examiner comments.

Write a review of a music CD with which you are familiar. [20]

Student 1

Im going to write a review of Michael Jacksons CD Thriller, I think this is a great album and my favorite from Jacko. I like it because it has some great songs in it and I like dancing to them.

I think it is better than his other albums because he does diferent things in this album and it makes me happy to listen to it and remember all the good things about him now he has died, I was really sorry that he died and I cried for a long time. I watched the funeral on TV and it was so moving with all his brothers there.

I think he was a good man whatever the papers say about the way he treated his children and all that fuss about holding his baby out of the window. I think the newspapers made too much of a fuss about that. He only did it as a joke he didnt men any harm by it. Thriller is a really good album. It has nine tracks which all have diferent beats and the words are interesting as well. It is my favorite album and I've got all his albums.

Content and organisation

Strong points

- There is a clear recommendation.

Weak points

- We do not learn much about what is on the album.
- The review wanders away from task when the student writes about the funeral and Michael Jackson's problems with the newspapers.
- The review is short.

Sentence structure, punctuation and spelling

Strong points

- The review uses paragraphs.

Weak points

- The student misspelled some words (for example, 'favourite' 'different').
- Commas are used instead of full stops (for example, in the first paragraph).
- Sentence structures are very similar (for example, 'I think…' is used a number of times).
- The student sometimes missed apostrophes: 'I'm', 'Jackson's', 'didn't'.

Student 2

Girls Aloud
Out of Control

This is another fabulous offering from the best girls group in the business! Manufactured bands usually don't last long but Girls Aloud have managed to capture the hearts of a growing group of admirers because they have good looks and good tunes.

Xenomania wrote and produced the album with their brilliant understanding for what will sell and the girls have done them proud. The first track 'The Promise' is a super starter that gets more enjoyable every time you listen to it. On the disc you can hear a cathedral choir and farm yard noises, this shows just how imaginative the producers are.

The best track is 'The Loving Kind' which was partly written by Pet Shop Boys and Xenomania. It's both sad and terrific to dance to which is unusual in the pop world, the most surprising track is 'Love is a Pain' with its solo from Cheryl Cole ('It don't matter to me, just be faithful to me'). Many think this was for Ashley who had cheated on her just before the albums release. She sounds really sad in this number.

If you are looking for great dance music their is the up-beat 'Miss You Bow Wow' with its brilliant chorus and some really odd lyrics. Girls Aloud have not lost there ability to sing stuff which gets the feet tapping and you out of your chair.

Perhaps this album isnt as great as 'Chemistry' or 'Tangled Up' but it's still one of the best to be produced this year and it deserves to be successful. Perhaps now all those people who were too snobbish to want to listen to a manufactured band will see them for what they are – a talented and beautiful group of professionals.

Examiner comments

Content and organisation

Strong points
- The student shows good knowledge of the subject.
- The student writes about individual tracks.
- The review is interesting to read
- A clear opinion is expressed.
- Vocabulary is varied.
- The work uses paragraphs.

Weak points
- The review could be a little longer.

Sentence structure, punctuation and spelling

Strong points
- Spelling is accurate.
- Punctuation is mostly accurate.
- Sentence structures are varied.

Weak points
- The student confuses 'there' and 'their'.
- The student missed an apostrophe: 'isn't'.
- Commas are sometimes used instead of full stops (for example, in the second paragraph).

Reviews: how to improve your response

- Remember you are the expert in this work. Write a review that will help a reader who probably does not know as much as you to make a decision about whether they want to read the book, watch the film or TV programme, or buy the CD.
- Remember in a review you must interest your reader. Humour will help you to do this. Be as lively and entertaining as you can.
- You will be able to choose what you review. Make sure it is something you know something about and have strong opinions on. You may love or hate the thing you are reviewing.
- You will get more marks if you include details in your review.
- Remember, you are being asked to give a personal opinion. Make sure your opinion is clear and give reasons for it.
- You can make reference to other CDs, films, books and TV programmes but make sure you write mostly about your choice.
- Remember to write enough: see the answer opposite for guidance on length. Short answers do not achieve C grades.
- Give your review a title and use paragraphs.
- Always check your work to get rid of careless errors.

Putting it into practice

- Find a review of a book, film, television programme or CD that you know in a newspaper or magazine.
- Examine the review and note down the things that the writer likes and dislikes.
- Look at the way the reviewer has introduced the review.
- Think about how the review ends.
- Make a list of things that you have learned from reading the review.
- Discuss your findings with a partner.

Your learning

This lesson will help you to:

- practise using key features of reviews
- develop a secure approach to writing a review.

When writing a review keep in mind that you:

- need to be lively and interesting
- need to be the expert – make sure that you show you are
- need to be fairly detailed in your review
- need a clear opening and that you make your recommendation at the end
- can review something you don't like.

Activity 1

Select a question from the three exam tasks below, and write your own review.

Write a review of a book you have read lately and really enjoyed. [20]

Write a review of a film you have seen. [20]

Write a review of television programme you have watched recently. [20]

Write a review of a music CD you have in your collection or on your iPod. [20]

In your review you may like to think about the following:

- *an introduction giving the reader some of the details the book, film, television programme or CD you are reviewing*
- *things you liked about the book, film, television programme or CD*
- *aspects you were less impressed with*
- *a conclusion in which you give your final judgement.*

Check your answer to Activity I. Use the mark scheme on pages 106 and 107.

- Did you choose your subject carefully?
- Did you provide a title?
- Did you write an interesting and lively opening?
- In giving information about the book/film/ television programme/CD were you careful not to give too much away?
- Did you include a conclusion where you make your opinions clear?
- Did you take care to check your work to get rid of the mistakes?
- How could you improve your review?

What is controlled assessment?

Your GCSE examination is made up of two parts:

- external assessment – the examination for Paper 1 and Paper 2
- controlled assessment – where your teacher will give you details of your tasks for Unit 3 and Unit 4.

For all of your written controlled assessment, you will be given the tasks in advance and your teacher will provide guidance. You will have an opportunity to study for them. Your teacher will tell you how much time you have to prepare for each task.

When you write your final version, you will be in 'controlled conditions'. This means there will be a time limit and you will not be allowed to discuss your work with other students or your teacher. In the Reading assignments you will be allowed to have clean copies of the texts you are writing about plus one A4 sheet of notes to help you. These notes must not contain a draft essay or an essay plan. In the Writing assignments you will not be allowed to have any notes. For both Reading and Writing assignments you will not be allowed access to dictionaries or thesauri. You can complete your work on a word processor but you must not have access to spell checker or grammar programmes. At this stage, your teacher will not be able to help you. Once you have finished your work you will not be able to change it, so you must take great care to do your best.

What is it worth?

Your controlled assessment is worth 60 per cent of your marks, so it is important that you do well if you want to get a good mark.

What does controlled assessment for GCSE English look like?

Unit 3: Literary texts and open writing

What is it worth? Unit 3 is worth 40 per cent of your marks: 20 per cent for reading and 20 per cent for writing.

What is assessed in reading?
You will need to write:

- an essay that makes links between a Shakespeare play and poetry chosen from the WJEC Poetry Collection (this is worth 10 per cent of your marks and you will have 4 hours to complete this work)
- an essay on a Different Cultures prose text (this is worth 10 per cent of your marks and you will have 2 hours to complete this work).

What is assessed in writing?
You will need to write:

- one piece of first-person writing
- one piece of third-person writing.

You will have two hours to complete both pieces of work.
General titles will be given to you for these tasks.

Unit 4: Speaking and Listening

What is it worth? Unit 4 is worth 20 per cent of your marks.

What is assessed?
Your speaking and listening skills will be tested in three ways. You will have to:

- give an individual presentation to a group
- take part in group discussion
- show your skill in role play.

The tasks will cover the following areas:

- communicating and adapting language
- interacting and responding
- creating and sustaining roles.

What does controlled assessment for GCSE English Language look like?

Unit 3: Literary reading and creative writing

What is it worth? Unit 3 is worth 30 per cent of your marks: 15 per cent for reading and 15 per cent for writing.

What is assessed in reading?
The reading part of your assessment is known as 'Studying written language'. You will need to write an essay on a play or a novel. This is worth 15 per cent of your marks. You will be given 2 hours to complete this task and your teacher will explain the task to you.

What is assessed in writing?
The writing part of your assessment is known as 'Using language'. You will need to write:
- one piece of descriptive writing (this is worth 7.5 per cent of your marks)
- one piece of narrative/expressive writing (this is worth 7.5 per cent of your marks).

You will have 2 hours to complete these two pieces.

General titles will be given to you for these tasks.

Unit 4: Using language (Speaking and Listening) and Studying spoken language

What is it worth? Unit 4 is worth 30 per cent of your marks: 20 per cent for Speaking and Listening, and 10 per cent for Studying spoken language.

What is assessed in Speaking and Listening?
Your speaking and listening skills will be tested in three ways. It is worth 20 per cent of your marks. You will have to:
- give an individual presentation to a group
- take part in group discussion
- show your skill in role play.

The tasks will cover the following areas:
- communicating and adapting language
- interacting and responding
- creating and sustaining roles.

What is assessed in Studying spoken language?
You will need to produce an essay on an aspect of spoken language (variations, choices or change in spoken language). This work could be on your own or others' use of spoken language and is worth 10 per cent of the total mark.

If you are taking English Language, support for Studying spoken language can be found on pages 152–171 of this book.

4 Studying spoken language

What is involved in Studying spoken language?
- You will study change, choice or variation in spoken language.
- This work could be on your own use of spoken language, or the spoken language of others.
- You will use a recording, transcript or memory of spoken language for your task.

How will this book help you?
Your teacher will:
- advise whether you are working with change, choice or variation in spoken language
- give you guidance on whether to use a recording, transcript or recollection for your task.

This section provides examiner guidance and a brief guide on:
- how to go about making a recording, transcript or recollection of spoken language
- what change, choice and variation in spoken language means, and some of the key features of each
- the processes and preparation a task might involve, using examples
- sample work so you can assess your own work in light of these
- examiner guidance and comments that will help you improve your marks.

What is language change, choice and variation?
- Language **change** is about how language changes to fit different contexts. For example, we do not speak the same way in a playground as we do in a doctor's surgery.
- Language **choice** is about how we choose our language to suit specific listeners. For example, we do not speak to a toddler in the way we speak to an adult.
- Language **variation** is about how we vary our use of standard and non-standard language, and reflect regional or specialist language. For example, we may include slang when speaking with friends but are more likely to use formal, standard English when speaking to a headteacher.

There is more on language change, choice and variation from page 160 onwards in this section.

How is a recording, transcript or recollection of spoken language used?
Capturing spoken language will help you to understand and explain key features of language.
- You may **record** language using simple recording devices or notes.
- You may make a **transcript** of language. A transcript is spoken language written down. You use symbols to show how things are said as well as what is said.
- You may use language recollection (memory) of language. This is where you build up a store of information and examples of language in use.

There is more on capturing spoken language from pages 154–159 onwards in this section.

How will my work be assessed?
Your work will be assessed through an essay in controlled conditions. It is worth 10 per cent of your marks. You will be assessed against Assessment Objective 2.
- Understand variations in spoken language, explaining why language changes in relationship to contexts.
- Assess the impact of spoken language choices in their own and others' use.

What will I need to do?

Research and planning

- Your teacher will give you details of your task and can give you general guidance and advice.
- You will have around 8 hours to gather information and spoken language samples.
- You may work with recordings, transcripts and language recollection.
- You may explore the features of language change, choice and variation.

Write an essay

- You will write an essay under formal supervision using the information and examples you have gathered.
- You will have 2 hours to write your final essay.
- You will have your notes with you.
- Your essay will be handed in with any notes or transcripts at the end of 2 hours.

What do studying spoken language tasks look like?

Below are examples of the general types of tasks.
Your teacher will give you details of your own specific task.

How spoken language is used different contexts

Candidates reflect on and explain their own and others' uses of language in some of the following situations:

- in the workplace
- on television
- in the classroom
- problem solving (giving directions, explaining a procedure, making decisions).

> This task is about **language change** – the way we change our language depending on the context of where we are. Your teacher will mark your work looking at how well you understand how the situation affects the words and voice of the speakers.

How spoken language is adapted to different listeners

Candidates explore how their own and others' use of language is adapted in the contexts of wider language use and variation. The following situations would provide appropriate contexts:

- responding to older or younger listeners
- responding to people in authority
- talking to peers and family
- responding to strangers.

> This task is about **language choice** – the way we choose how we speak depending on who the listener is. Your teacher will mark your work looking at how well you can explain how words and voices are chosen and shaped for different listeners.

The effects of choices in the use of standard and non-standard forms of spoken language

Candidates demonstrate their understanding of the reasons for and effects of these choices, and how they may vary over time and place. The following situations would provide appropriate contexts:

- using non-standard forms to peers and family
- using standard forms to strangers and those in authority
- the effects of standard and non-standard forms in television and radio advertising.

> This task is about **language variation** – the way we use standard and non-standard forms of language, and reflect regional or specialist language. Your teacher will mark your work looking for whether you can recognise standard and non-standard speech and appreciate their effects.

Your learning

This lesson will help you to:

- understand how to make a record of spoken language
- make your own record of spoken language.

Recording spoken language will help you to understand and explain key features of language.

Recording language

It is often best to make a recording with a mobile phone, cassette recorder or a special recording device. This means that:

- you will have a permanent record and can replay it as many times as you like
- you will have an accurate recording of speech, so you will hear not just *what* people say but *how* they say it
- you can record from real life, television or radio: sports commentary, chat shows, radio phone-ins and quiz shows all work well.

Activity 1

1 Try out your own recording of language.

Record a small group of boys and a small group of girls. Find out how males and females talk differently. Ask them to discuss the following statement for around 2 minutes:

'Are females or males the most polite?'

2 Make sure your recording is useful. Use a checklist like the one below.

Making a good recording

✓ Make sure you have the permission of the group.
✓ Make sure you have enough recording space on your device.
✓ Don't have too big a group – too many voices can be confusing.
✓ Keep the recording device near the people speaking.
✓ If the group is uncomfortable at first, start when they have relaxed.
✓ Make the recording in a quiet place, if that is possible.

Capturing the sample you need

✓ Give the group something definite to discuss.
✓ Take your recording somewhere quiet and replay it.
✓ Choose the sections that are most useful for your task.
✓ Note down anything to improve next time. For example: Can you hear everything or do you need to be closer to the speaker? Do you need to cut out background noise?

3   Now take information from your recording. You may need to listen to it a number of times. Complete a table like the one below. Compare your results. What do they tell you?

Features of politeness	Male	Female
Polite		
Polite words – please, thanks, you're welcome, OK,	Thanks, yes ok	Please
Uses 'we' and 'don't you think'? to include others	We – twice Innit – three times	We – used five times Don't we – three times
Compliments – great, lovely, good idea, nice, smashing		Lovely
Not polite		
Interrupts others	///	//
Negative comments – rubbish, that's a terrible idea	/	///

Use a tick ✓ or tally mark / to help you keep count.

Recording language using instant notes

You can also record language using instant notes. These can be useful if you are listening for one or two language features. You can log these more easily straight into a well-planned table that will:

- be easy to use
- record information about the speakers
- record something about the situation.

Activity 2

1   Try making instant notes about spoken language. You could make notes to help with your own controlled assessment task, or use the task below.

    Give a small group of boys and a small group of girls around 2 minutes to discuss the following.

- What do boys talk about?
- What do girls talk about?

2   Complete a table like the one below. Comment on your findings.

Group gender m/f	Names used by the group	Subject discussed
M	Boys, mun, guys, lads	Football teams, money
F	Babes, guys, girls, mun	Food, films, fashion
M and F		

Using a transcript

Your learning

This lesson will help you to:

- understand some key features of a transcript
- make your own transcript.

A transcript is spoken language written down, so it is easier to see the features and make comments.

Activity 1

1 Spoken language does not always fall easily into sentences. It has its own rules, so we use slightly different tools. Compare the following examples of written and spoken language. What do you learn from the transcript that you do not learn from the written version?

Pause of 2 seconds as customer decides.	Extra stress on type of drink shown by underlined word.	Other effects such as coughs or smiles are shown in brackets.

Written language

C: A can of coke please.

S: Diet coke or regular coke?

C: Regular please.

S: That's sixty-five pence.

C: No, I want two cans.

S: That's one pound thirty then.

Spoken language

C: Er (2) can of coke please

S: Diet or regular?

C: (2) <u>Regular</u> please

S: sixty five p then please (coughs)

C: No, I want <u>two</u> cans

S: (tut) (.) that'll be one thirty then

Shopkeeper overlaps and interrupts the customer.	Extra stress on number of cans.

We can see in the transcript how important the pauses are, that the shopkeeper 'tuts' with the change of order showing irritation, and the underlined words show where words are stressed. It is much more difficult to show these features in a 'written' version.

2 Now look at the statement below.

No, I'm not going to London tomorrow.

When this statement is spoken, the use of pauses and emphasis on different words can change its meaning. Read the two transcripts of the statement below, for example. The changed meaning is shown in italics.

- No, I'm not going to London <u>tomorrow</u>. (*I'm going the day after*)
- (smiles) No, <u>I'm</u> not going to London tomorrow. (*Someone else is, I got out of it*)

3 Speak the statement in another way to show a different meaning.

Look at the table below showing symbols used in transcripts.

Key transcript symbols

Symbol	What the symbol means	What the symbol tells us
(.)	Pause	Usually less than half a second long. We use them in our speech to punctuate what we say and to give ourselves time to think Oh(.)right(.) ok then(.)
(2)	Pause in seconds	Check the longer pauses. Usually they mean something is going on such as waiting for a reply or thinking.
Underlined word(s)	Emphasis	Have a close look at why these words have been given extra emphasis.
(coughs)	Other noises	Other contextual details.
( )	Unidentifiable speech	Used when you really can't make out what was said.
C, S	Initial of speaker	In the example on the opposite page, C for customer, S for shopkeeper.

Activity 2

Now try out your own transcript. It could be related to your controlled assessment task or another sample. See the example on page 160. Follow the steps below.

Step 1: Make/select a clear recording of spoken language. If you have a choice of recordings, start with the one with fewest voices – it is easier.

Step 2: Choose carefully which part of your recording you are going to transcribe. It needs to be clear and include the features you are explaining. If it is your first transcript, select no more than 30 seconds.

Step 3: Writing it down needs time and patience. Use headphones or ear pieces if you have them. Work on only five seconds of recording at a time, less if you need to. Listen carefully and replay the recording as often as you need to get an accurate transcript.

Step 4: Make your transcript. Choose key transcript symbols from the box.

Step 5: Think carefully or discuss with your teacher the kinds of spoken language features that you will be looking out for.

Step 6: Use a highlighter to pick out features you might want to comment on. It is usually helpful to look for common speech features such as:
questions – for example, 'Ravi, where were you on Monday?'
commands – for example, 'settle down'
politeness – for example, 'page 37 please'
topic setting – for example, 'We were doing the D-Day landings'
hesitation – for example, 'Sir, (erm) (.)'.

Using spoken language

Spoken language recollection (or memory) is where you use your and other people's knowledge of speech so that you can build up a store of information and examples used by different people in many different situations.

You will get the best range of words, information and language use if you can ask a variety of different people: old, young, male, female, local people and people in other parts of the country.

Activity 1

1 Try working with language recollection in a way that helps with your own controlled assessment task, or use the tasks below.

- Find out the different words/phrases people use to describe how they feel when they are really pleased or really fed up.

- Find out the different words people use to describe a specific item. Choose items that most interest you or you could try from the following: friend, bread roll, mid-morning snack, a foolish person, bad tempered, attractive.

2 You could use language recollection to gather the information you need in a number of ways.

- Talk with your friends and family. Notice the phrases they use that you want to collect. Make a note of them as quickly as possible afterwards.

- Discuss words in a group. Share and note down words and phrases. Working in a group can help you record more.

- Use the Internet, especially if you belong to a social networking site and know people who might use different words/phrases in different areas of the country.

3 Create a table so that you can log the variations of words and phrases. You could structure your findings like the table below.

Standard English	Grandparents/ older person	Parents/ guardians	Your friends	Local word	My words
Pleased	Glad, happy, thrilled	Beaming, landed	Chuffed, well happy, stoked, made up	Landed	
To truant	Mitch, bunk off	Bunk off, truant	Do a bunk, hookey, skip	Mitch	
Friend					

When you explore words/phrases, watch out for the way language varies. You might find examples of language like the ones below. If so, you could note this down on your table.

✓ **Language affected by where you live**: the way people speak often reflects where they live. This can lead to:
  - different accents (the sound of words), for example Cockney, West Country, Geordie
  - different dialects (groups of words that can be special to a region), for example 'nesh', 'mardy' – used in Lancashire to mean 'weak' and 'complaining'.

✓ **New meanings for old words**: 'mouse' has a new meaning now, as do 'chip', 'Mac', 'wireless' and 'mega'. Fifty years ago a wireless referred to a radio.

✓ **New words for new inventions**: we now have a Nokia, a Dyson®, an iPod, downloads, uploads and Facebook.

✓ **Language created for fun**: for example, young people create and use slang words such as 'wicked', 'sick', 'mint', just as the generations before them had 'bad', 'groovy' and 'hip'.

Your table may be a useful source of spoken language recollection for your controlled assessment task.

Examiner tips

- When you ask people about words and phrases they may just repeat the words used in the question. For example, if you ask for the word they used for playing truant, they may say 'playing truant'. Instead try asking, 'What did you used to call it when you or someone else took a day off school without permission?'
- Older people and parents may want to give you only the standard English words. Emphasise that you want local words and informal words.
- Ask people to tell you as many words as they can.

Your learning

This lesson will help you to:

- understand how spoken language changes in different contexts
- analyse a transcript and explain how language changes.

When we talk about **language change** we are talking about how we change our language depending on the context we are in. For example, we don't speak in the playground in the same way as we do in a doctor's surgery. To explain how language changes in context it is useful to explore situations that strongly affect the way language is used. Here is a brief example of the kind of approach you might take with language change, using the following sample task.

Explain how teachers use spoken language in the classroom. [20]

Answer the questions opposite about the transcript below.

The class takes place in a secondary school, first lesson of the day on a Tuesday. It is a history lesson for Year 11 pupils both male and female. T = teacher, S1, S2, S3 – students in the class.

T: <u>Right everyone, settle down</u> (.) settle down (.) Are we all here then?(.) Ok. (1) Ravi, where were <u>you</u> on Monday? (.) Not like you to be off (.) Nothing to do with the <u>homework</u> was it?

S1:   <u>No</u> sir

T: (.) OK then class (.) Let's see what you've remembered. We were doing the <u>D-Day landings</u> or <u>Overlord</u> to give it its code-name. The British, the Americans and Canadian marines took part in the biggest sea-borne invasion <u>ever</u>. But what <u>year</u> were the D-Day landings? (.) Jamie?

S2: Sir, (erm) (.) 1938?

T: No, <u>not quite</u> Jamie, as World War II hadn't even <u>started</u> then! Sara?

S3: Sir was it 1944?

T: Yes it was Sara, very good.

Examiner tips

Always ask these questions when you look how language changes in a specific location or situation.

- What kind of language is expected in your chosen context?
- What kind of behaviour is expected there?
- Who is likely to have control over the subject and speak the most?
- Is there a special vocabulary or group of words the speakers use?

Activity 1

Use these questions to explore the transcript opposite. The questions in bold are useful for exploring language change in any context.

1 What effect does the situation or context have here? Classrooms have unwritten rules that everyone follows, like not shouting out. Can you suggest some more?

2 Who sets the topic? How does the teacher signal that the lesson is about to start, and get it going in the right direction?

3 Which words used here are special to the subject? For example historical terms such as 'D-Day landings' and 'battle'. Can you find two more?

4 Who uses questions? Who uses the most questions in the transcript opposite? How many?

5 Who uses commands and how are they used? Teachers usually make their commands and their ways of saying 'wrong' polite, for example 'not quite'. Why do you think that is?

6 Pauses are important – what do they say? Find examples of pauses used by the teacher. Why do you think they have been used?

Activity 2

1 Read GradeStudio on pages 162–163. It has two answers to the sample task opposite along with examiner comments. Compare the differences between typical E and C grade responses.

2 Use everything you have learned to improve your response in your own controlled assessment task. Remember:

- you are advised to write about 400 words
- you must express ideas and information clearly, precisely and accurately
- introductory paragraph: say something about the effect of the situation on the spoken language
- central paragraphs: work your way through the transcript making comments on how the language is used in context, pick out key features
- final paragraph: draw together your ideas and make some cautious conclusions.

Examiner tips

Watch out for the following key things to help improve your response.

- **Show your understanding of language change.** How the context affects the vocabulary and voice of the speakers.
- **Use quotations** to support your main points.
- **Say *what* is happening but also *why* it is happening.** For example, 'He asks lots of questions' is true. 'He asks lots of questions so the class have to pay attention as they might be next', will get you higher marks.
- **Develop the answer.** For example, you could say: 'This is a lot for the students to take in', but you need to say more than this. For example: 'This is a lot for the students to take in so he is quite gentle when they get it wrong'. Follow this up with some supporting quotation, for example 'No, <u>not quite</u> Jamie'.
- Words such as 'could' and 'might' can help you make useful comments about language. For example: Jamie gets the answer wrong and the teacher says 'No, <u>not quite</u> Jamie'. This *could* be sarcastic or the teacher *might* be saying 'close but not quite right'.

GradeStudio

Here are two student responses to the exam task below. Read the answers and the examiner comments.

Explain how the teacher uses spoken language in the classroom. [20]

Student 1

this opening is not wrong but it mostly just describes the events

better use of quotation: could the teacher have a different reason for telling them?

some grasp of the main ideas, but it is too general

From the opening of the essay

In the classroom the teacher is the boss. He wants to get the lesson started and get on with the subject. I think that he is annoyed that everyone is being noisy and he wants them to be quiet. That is why he
5 picks on Ravi. He quickly asks who is not there and tells Ravi off for missing the last lesson. Ravi says that he did do his homework.

From the middle paragraphs of the essay

The teacher tells the whole class what they are studying as they might not have remembered. *We were doing the <u>D-Day landings</u> or <u>Overlord</u> to give*
10 *it its code-name.* He asks lots of questions. This one is about the D-Day landings. *But what <u>year</u> were the D-Day landings? Jamie?*
Jamie gets the answer wrong so the teacher moves on to Sara.

From the ending of the essay

The teacher gives a lot of facts in this lesson. This is a lot for the
15 students to take in. The students get a lot of facts wrong and the teacher corrects them. Sara gets closest to giving a correct answer.

Examiner comments

Strong points
- Some focus on the teacher's use of questions (lines 4, 10).
- Better support by quotation in the middle of the essay (lines 9, 10, 11).
- Some awareness of the effect of the situation, for example the classroom (lines 1, 14, 15).

Weak points
- The writing is too general: 'The students get a lot of facts wrong' (line 15). More detail is needed: for example, 'Jamie gets the date of the D-Day landings wrong'.
- The comments have been made too quickly. For example, 'That is why he picks on Ravi' (lines 4, 5). More thought is needed. Is the teacher picking on Ravi? Or might it be because the class is noisy?
- There is not enough focus on speech. Very little has been said about the pauses or the emphasised words, for example how the teacher speaks loudly at the start to get attention but then mainly speaks loudly on key words like *<u>Overlord</u>* and when he comments on answers like 'not quite' and 'very good'.

Student 2

quite a good opening – some useful points on the purpose of the text

some better understanding here and evidence in support, but the student misses the important pause (.) between the question and the choice of who should answer

some sensible summing up but short on examples: the reason given for the teacher talking the most is not the best one or the only one

From the opening of the essay

In the classroom the teacher wants to be in control so that everybody learns. So he speaks loudly and repeats himself <u>*Right everyone, settle down*</u> *(.) settle down.* The pupils probably want an easy lesson. The teacher makes
5 sure that the class gets ready to learn by saying *We were doing the <u>D-Day</u> <u>landings</u> or <u>Overlord</u> to give it its code-name. The British, the Americans and Canadian marines took part in the biggest sea-borne invasion <u>ever</u>.* He gives enough information to remind the students of what they were learning.

From the middle paragraphs of the essay

10 Once he has got the students involved he throws out a question. *But what year were the D-Day landings? Jamie?* This keeps the students on their toes. Jamie is unsure, he says *erm* then gets the answer wrong. The teacher moves on to Sara who gets the answer. But some students might feel left out as he only praises Sara. He should give more of them a chance to
15 answer.

From the ending of the essay

Overall the teacher chooses language to create a good mood and adapts his language so that the students can understand him. The teacher talks the most because he knows the most. He asks lots of questions to see if the class know what they are talking about and have done their homework.

Examiner comments

Strong points

- There is a good focus on spoken language features such as emphasis (line 3), repetition (line 3) and questions (lines 10, 11).
- The focus on the context of the classroom is strong: getting ready to learn (lines 1, 8), the purpose of praise (line 11).
- There is emphasis on the mood of the lesson. For example, line 13.

Weak points

- No evidence is given: 'The pupils probably want an easy lesson.' There is nothing to back this up.
- Comments on the features of speech are missing: 'But what <u>year</u> were the D-Day landings? Jamie?' misses out the vital pause (.)
- The writing is a bit too general: 'He asks lots of questions'. This is sometimes true, but not always. Better to write, 'Twice he asks questions to check up on the class's knowledge' and then give examples.

Language change: how to improve your response

- Be specific about how the situation is having an effect on the type of language used. Give examples and back them up with quotations. Then develop your comments.
- Show how the rules of the situation are affecting speech through features such as emphasis, repetition and pause.

Putting it into practice

In the future:
- focus on the spoken language features
- use evidence to support the points you make.

Language choice

- understand how we choose language for different listeners
- analyse a transcript and show the importance of language choice.

When we talk about **language choice** we are talking about how we choose our language depending on who the listener is. For example, we don't speak to toddlers in the same way we speak to adults. We choose our language carefully.

Here is a brief example of the kind of approach you might take with language choice, using the following sample task.

Show that you understand the significance of the language choices made for different listeners. [20]

In this sample we are working with a transcript made from a recording. Read the transcript, then answer the questions opposite.

> The transcript is of an interview between a parent and a headteacher. The parent has brought her son with her; he seems uninterested in the discussion. The headteacher has the administrator with her. It is lunchtime.
>
> **Headteacher:** (quietly to the administrator) I can tell this parent's going to be a pain (.) try and get some really good facts (.) throw her off ok (3)
> **Administrator:** ok
> **HT:** (very quietly) waste of time. (3) (louder) Miss Lovering (.) hello
> 5 **Parent:** (to son) sit down (1) I am here today because I am appalled at the standard of food served in your school
> **HT:** well I don't serve any food in this school which is why I've brought my colleague along Alex Bradley-Hooters
> **Parent:** well maybe he can explain then
> 10 **Administrator:** our food is of high quality from (.) trusted and (.) inspected farmers around the country the food (.) the food is pre-prepared and brought in
> **Parent:** huh
> **Administrator:** in vacuum packs to ensure freshness (1)
> **HT:** there you have it it's absolutely perfect food there's not a problem

Always ask these key questions of language choice.
- What different language choices are made by different speakers?
- Why do they make them?
- Who changes their speech most to suit the listener?
- Does anyone seem to speak down or raise their speech level?
- Who seems most comfortable in the discussion? Who seems most awkward?

Activity 1

Use these questions to explore the transcript opposite. The questions in bold are useful for exploring language choice in any context.

1   **What effects do the language choices of the speakers have?** The headteacher speaks in two quite different ways. For example, she speaks quietly to the administrator 'waste of time'. What language choice does she make in line 7? Why?

2   **How is the seriousness of the topic signalled by the word choice of the speakers?** The parent's language choice is quite formal. For example, the parent says 'I am here today' – announcing herself. Can you pick out another example of her formal language?

3   **Confidence and fluent language.** Very often confident people speak fluently and those lacking confidence people speak hesitantly and pause more.

   - Can you identify the most nervous person here?
   - How does the parent make it clear that she is less than impressed?

Watch out for key things to help improve your marks.
- **Use quotations** to support your main points.
- **Say *what* is happening but also *why* something is happening.** For example, 'The mother speaks in a formal way: "well maybe he can explain then", can be improved by adding 'She does this to show she is not afraid of the head teacher'.
- **Develop the answer.** You could say: 'The headteacher talks just as formally as the parent.' You could say more: 'She needs to show she is taking the situation seriously.' Follow this up with some supporting quotation, for example, 'Well I don't serve any food in this school which is why I've brought my colleague along.'

GradeStudio

Here is a student response to the exam task below. Read the answer and the examiner comments.

Show that you understand the significance of the language choices made for different listeners. [20]

Extract typical of an E / grade answer

Student 1

From the opening of the essay
The headteacher and the administrator know they are in for trouble so they take sides against the mother. They are a bit scared because they whisper. The mother has come in to complain about the food that her son has to eat and she brings her son with her so he can back her up! Perhaps they come at lunch time so they can see the rubbish food.

From the middle paragraphs of the essay
The mother sounds quite posh when she complains as she wants to impress the headteacher. She is angry too and she won't be fooled by excuses. The son doesn't help her much as he doesn't say anything.

From the ending of the essay
The administrator takes over as he can see the headteacher is struggling. He sounds like he knows what he is talking about and is definitely trying to impress the mother. But then we see it isn't working because the parent says 'Huh'. The headteacher takes over again and tries to impress the parent but she isn't very convincing because she doesn't know much about food. We don't know who wins the argument but it's probably the headteacher.

> this student does look at the scene in a simple way

> simple idea of the way the mother speaks here

> some ideas here on how the administrator tries to impress

Examiner comments

Strong points
- Some understanding of the influences on speaker's choices.
- This answer is clear on some of the language choices and offers a reason for their speaking quietly.
- There is some understanding of the mother's complaint. The answer makes some attempts to describe language choices though in a simple way, 'quite posh' (line 8).
- This answer looks simply at language choices and reasons for them.

Weak points
- There is very little quotation to support the ideas.
- Ideas are not developed.

Student 2

From the opening of the essay
The head teacher and the administrator have the authority here and they plot together before they start to talk to the parent, *try and get some really good facts(.) throw her off OK.*

> quotation and attention to how the teacher speaks (quietly), good start

5 The mother has come in to complain about the food that her son has to eat and the two school employees are ganging up to tell her that everything is OK. The head teacher speaks very quietly which shows he may be a bit scared.

From the middle paragraphs of the essay
10 The mother uses quite posh English to make her complaint, *I am appalled at the standard of food served in your school.* The head teacher replies in just as posh a way by observing that she has nothing to do with the food which drops her colleague right in it!

> 'posh English' is all right; 'formal English' would be better

From the ending of the essay
15 The administrator tries to impress the mother with the quality of the food, and some special words that make him sound expert *high quality from trusted and inspected farmers around the country, ... the food is pre-prepared and brought in.* The head teacher follows up *it's absolutely perfect food* and the mother has to give in.

> a judgement is made, the parent loses but is this the end?

Examiner comments

Strong points
- Attention given to how people speak (lines 7, 10).
- The administrator's use of 'special words' is identified.

Weak points
- Speaking quietly does not mean that the headteacher is 'scared' (line 8).
- 'Posh English' would be better identified as 'formal' or 'Standard English'.

Language choice: how to improve your response
- Focus your essay on the language choices of the main speakers. What is influencing these choices?
- Show that you understand why certain words are chosen in relationship to the listeners. A typical Grade G response will show 'limited' understanding. A typical Grade E response will show 'some' understanding, while for a typical Grade C the understanding of the choices will be 'clear'.
- Use quotations to support what you say. Even short quotes like 'appalled' and 'huh' will improve your answer.

Putting it into practice

In the future:
- use quotations to support what you say
- focus your answer on the main speakers.

Language variation

When we talk about **language variation** we are talking about how we vary between standard and non-standard ways of speaking. For example, we might use slang with friends and formal language with a teacher. We might speak in dialect. Language use can be very varied. An important variation is between standard or non-standard spoken language.

- **Non-standard language** tends to be used with family and friends. It is often informal and may include slang or dialect words.

- **Standard language** tends to be used with strangers, those in authority or in situations that are formal, such as interviews. It is more formal and polite.

Here is a brief example of the kind of approach you might take with language variation, using the following sample task.

Choose a situation where the use of a standard or non-standard language variety is important. Explain why speakers may use standard and non-standard language at different times and places.

Activity 1

Read the transcripts opposite. They show how a speaker has chosen to vary her use of non-standard and standard forms to suit a different time and place.

Explore the way the language has been varied by completing a table like the one opposite.

Pair up the non-standard language used in the school playground with the standard language used in the classroom.

Examiner tips

Always use the following key questions of language variation.
- How would you describe something to impress your best mates? The language you would use would be non-standard English.
- How might you say the same thing to impress your teacher or a stranger? That is very likely to be standard English.

Non-standard spoken language: Melissa, a Manchester schoolgirl, telling her friends about her work experience in the school playground at break.

aw yer (.) it were well good (.) they let me 'ave a go at all the jobs n'everything (.) and they treated me just like one o' them (.) I got to work in the office for a bit (.) then I was out on t'delivery van for a coupla days (1) that were top (.) then on the last day like they took me out to a well good restaurant cos I'd slaved away like (.) and they bought me lunch cos they said I were (.) like (.) one of them really and gave me a pressie (1) they said they might even have a job for me when I leave school (.) I had a bangin time it were great

Standard spoken language: Melissa telling her form teacher about her work experience in the classroom at the end of the lesson.

yes (.) I had a really good time Miss (.) they didn't just make me do photocopying (.) they let me try out all of the jobs and treated me like a proper worker (.) I really enjoyed it (.) I worked in the office for two days and then I had two days out on deliveries so I could experience that as well (.) I really enjoyed that (.) then on the last day they took me out for a lunch because they said I'd worked so hard and they weren't allowed to pay me and they gave me a present (.) some vouchers too (.) I really enjoyed it Miss (.) and they said they might even have a job for me when I leave school

Melissa to her friends	Melissa to her teacher	Type of variation
it were well good	I had a really good time Miss	Dialect 'it were' and 'well' instead of 'really'
they let me 'ave a go	they let me try out	Dropping the 'h' as part of the local accent
coupla	for two days	Shortened version of 'a couple of'
that were top	I really enjoyed that	Non-standard dialect
pressie	present	Shortened version

Here are two student responses to the exam task below. Read the answers and the examiner comments.

Choose a situation where the use of a standard or non-standard language variety is important. Explain why speakers may use standard and non-standard language at different times and places. [20]

Extract typical of an E grade answer

Student 1

> talks simply about the two situations; some quotation

From the opening of the essay

Melissa is a Manchester student who has been on work experience. First she tells her mates about it in the playground and then she goes on to tell her teacher later in the classroom. She seems really excited and she uses
5 lots of slang which is sloppy speech, like coupla. She talks like a teenager which is what she is. When she talks to her teacher she makes an effort to sound a bit more proper.

> the focus is too much on what she says and not how she is saying it

From the middle part of the essay

Melissa wants to impress her teacher with what she did on work experience
10 and how good the company thought she was. She wants her teacher to know she wasn't messing about. She keeps saying she really enjoyed it.

> some direct comparison and quotation; the best selection of this answer

From the end of the essay

Melissa must have enjoyed her work experience. She sounds really excited when she tells her friends but a bit calmer when she tells her teacher. She
15 is sort of showing off to her friends. She gets so excited she uses slang like pressie but to her teacher she says the proper word present.

Examiner comments

Strong points
- This candidate can describe the events and the two transcripts in a straightforward way.
- The candidate is aware of some differences in the language and can describe them in a straightforward way.

Weak points
- This candidate does not write very much on how the language Manjit uses varies.
- This candidate does not link the language used to the place in which the transcript was recorded.
- A better description than 'proper' or correct speech is standard English.

Student 2

offers a range of comments on Melissa's language

From the opening of the essay

In this transcript Melissa is talking to her friends about her work experience. She is quite excited about it and that is making her jumble her words and not speak properly. For example, she says *yer* not *yes*, which is
5 the language of the playground and is non-standard. She runs quite a lot of her words together. Maybe she just talks fast.

From the middle of the essay

some good selection of examples – good on wanting to impress

When she talks to her teacher in the classroom Melissa goes all posh (standard English). She seems to want to impress her teacher and is
10 quite polite, *miss*. She clearly can talk properly when she wants to. She doesn't shorten her words either, she says *present*, not *pressie* and uses harder words like *experience*.

From the end of the essay

misses the idea that Melissa can vary her language

Melissa says, *like* a lot which I suppose is a northern thing as they say it
15 on 'Coronation Street' but she doesn't say it to her teacher who would probably tell her off. Melissa's mates probably all talk like her so they would understand what she is saying.

Examiner comments

Strong points
- This student uses quite a lot of quotation to support ideas.
- She is broadly aware of the Manchester accent (although does not yet identify slang, accent or dialect).

Weak points
- She does not seem to realise though that Melissa, like everyone else, can vary her language to suit the situation.
- The candidate does not make it clear that you can impress some people by using standard language, and others by using non-standard.

Language variation: how to improve your response

- Focus your essay on the language varieties of the main speaker(s) and how they link to the time and place in which they are used.
- It is important to recognise that we all speak several varieties of English and that depending on the audience sometimes standard English impresses and sometimes non-standard does.
- Identify the difference between slang, accent and dialect.
- Find examples of non-standard and standard speech. Better still if you can find a pair of words or phrases, for example 'very good' (standard) versus 'dead good' (non-standard).

Putting it into practice

In the future:
- focus on the language of the main speakers
- use examples of the language to support the points you make.

Preparing for the exam

Reading paper

The **Resource Material** *on pages 174–175 is a leaflet that tries to encourage readers to visit Sandringham.*

The article opposite, 'A visit to Sandringham – holiday review', is a review that appeared on the Internet.

Look at the leaflet about Sandringham.

A1. *(a)* **How big are the gardens at Sandringham?** [1]

    (b) **List three of the vehicles to be found in the Sandringham museum.** [3]

    (c) **List three areas within the Visitor Centre.** [3]

    (d) **When was Sandringham House built?** [1]

    (e) **Which part of Sandringham House is open to the public?** [1]

    (f) **On which two days in the year is the Visitor Centre closed?** [1]

A2. **How does the leaflet try to attract visitors to Sandringham?**

You should write about:
- **the attractions mentioned**
- **words and phrases intended to persuade**
- **the choice of photographs.** [10]

A3. **What are the article writer's thoughts and feelings about the family's visit to Sandringham?**

You should include:
- **what she liked about the visit**
- **what she disliked**
- **her overall impression.** [10]

Use details and information from the leaflet and the article to answer the following question.

A4. **Both of these texts are about visiting Sandringham. Compare and contrast what the two texts say about:**
- **visiting the gardens and country park**
- **visiting the museum**
- **visiting the house.** [10]

A visit to Sandringham – holiday review

Any holiday in Norfolk would not be complete without a visit to Sandringham; at least that's what I told my daughter Lizzie, 16, and Tom, who's 7. They didn't seem immediately impressed by the prospect, but Tom was much more keen when I told him we might even get to see The Queen there.

The brochure I'd picked up made the place sound impressive, despite it being a typically rainy August day. I was pleased that getting to Sandringham was easy; it was well sign-posted and parking was free, always a bonus. However, it's a pricey day out: as Lizzie is 16, I had to pay for two £10 adult admission tickets and £5 for Tom. £25 family rates are available for a couple with up to three children, but it was the same price for me and my two children: a little unfair I thought.

When we got into the house, I was disappointed that so few of the rooms were actually open to the public, but the guides were happy to tell us about the house, and even Lizzie was interested to know about what the Royal Family do when they stay there. Tom was a bit bored by all the crockery on display, though I was pleased he liked seeing all the old guns and firearms, and the guide told him some interesting stories about which member of the royal family had used this shotgun or that rifle. When we went across into the museum, he was fascinated by the pedal car that had belonged to Prince Charles and this was perhaps the most interesting part of the day. There is a really good collection of old royal cars on show along with some fire engines and the royal Land Rover, which Tom was very keen to sit in. The museum also had a collection of stuffed animals but these made Lizzie very agitated and she began telling anyone within earshot why hunting was unfair and cruel. Oh, the joys of teenage children!

Out in the fresh air again, I enjoyed the gardens, but having said to the children we could take one of the advertised 'tractor tours' as a little extra treat, it was annoying to realise there were only limited places available and we were too late to book a trip. Though the children lost interest quickly, I loved seeing the collections of fuchsias and camellias and there were some very pretty areas like the summer house and the little waterfall and some interesting sculptures too.

We'd not taken a packed lunch but there was a self-service restaurant or the Stables Tearoom. There was plenty of choice and the food was good, though again it was all quite pricey and if I came again I would definitely take a picnic. The Gift Shop was full of all sorts of souvenirs, from tea towels and postcards of the royals to locally-produced jam and honey, which I thought made good reminders of our day there.

As we left, Tom said he wished he'd see The Queen, but Lizzie told him that was so unlikely as to be not worth considering. I felt that for adults interested in getting to find out more about the Royal Family it was a worthwhile, but expensive, half-day visit for a family but in truth, there's not much to occupy teenagers or young children. I made a mental note that I would come again, but on my own, if only to enjoy more of the wonderful gardens and grounds.

SANDRINGHAM

The Norfolk Retreat of Her Majesty The Queen

2009

OPEN DATES

House, Museum and Gardens
Saturday 11 April to Friday 24 July
Re-opens Sunday 2 August to Sunday 1 November
Open every day. Average time of visit: allow 3½ hours

Sandringham Visitor Centre
Open daily all year except Good Friday and Christmas Day

Accessibility

Wheelchair access throughout; helpers admitted free. Long distances involved; please ask in advance for access guide (01553 612908) or check the *Visiting Accessibility* page on **www.sandringhamestate.co.uk** for full details. Dogs, except registered assistance dogs, are not admitted in the Gardens but are welcome under close control in the Country Park.

HOURS

House 11 am to 4.45 pm (4 pm in October)
Museum 11 am to 5 pm (4 pm in October)
Gardens 10.30 am to 5 pm (4 pm in October)

GUIDED GARDEN TOURS

Public: Fridays and Saturdays at 11 am and 2 pm
Groups: by prior arrangement

PRICES

	House, Gardens & Museum	Gardens & Museum
Adult	£10.00	£6.50
Senior Citizen/Student	£8.00	£5.50
Child (5–15)	£5.00	£3.50
Family (2 adults & 3 children)	£25.00	£16.50
Season Ticket from £25.00		
Guided Garden Tour supplement: £2.50		

www.sandringhamestate.co.uk

Sandringham's website is the place to look for up-to-the-minute information. It includes our special events calendar, as well as full details of group discounts, a booking form and suggestions for planning your day, plus catering suggestions for groups of all sizes. Alternatively contact: Public Enterprises, The Estate Office, Sandringham, Norfolk PE35 6EN
TELEPHONE 01553 612908 **FAX** 01485 541571
EMAIL visits@sandringhamestate.co.uk

Neither a palace nor a castle, Sandringham is a country house with an atmosphere of welcome.

Built in 1870 by the Prince and Princess of Wales (later King Edward VII and Queen Alexandra), Sandringham has been passed down as a private home through four generations of British monarchs, and is now the country retreat of Her Majesty The Queen and His Royal Highness The Duke of Edinburgh. The main ground-floor rooms, regularly used by the Royal Family, are open to the public and the decor and contents, collected by many members of the Royal Family, remain very much as they were in Edwardian times.

VISITOR CENTRE

The Visitor Centre provides excellent facilities and is open all year. The timber buildings were designed to blend into the Norfolk heathland landscape.

- The self-service **Restaurant** is air-conditioned and seats 200. It offers a comprehensive range of snacks and meals. Lunches for groups are our speciality – contact us for seasonal menus.

- **Tractor and trailer tours** of the Country Park operate from April to October.

- **Gift Shop** specialising in British-made goods and exclusive Sandringham souvenirs, and a **Farm Shop** selling Estate-grown, local, rare breed and organic produce.

- **Plant Centre** selling houseplants, flowers, shrubs and herbaceous plants grown in the Sandringham glasshouses.

- **Sandringham Private Events** offer a wide range of services from conferences and marquee events to elegant dinners, all tailored by our experienced events team to suit our clients' individual requirements.

THE MUSEUM

Pride of place goes to the vintage Royal motor vehicles, including the first motor car owned by a member of the British monarchy, a 1900 Daimler Phaeton, and the splendid Merryweather Fire Engine which was used by the Estate's own Fire Brigade. Several children's cars are on display as well as carriages and the old Estate game cart.

King George V created his own private museum of big game trophies in rooms attached to the stable block and the remaining coach houses and stables have been converted to house a varied and ever-growing collection of objects. Among these are stunning Arts and Crafts ceramic tiles and plaques designed for the now-vanished Sandringham Dairy as well as commemorative china dating back to the reign of William IV.

Next to the Museum is the Stables Tearoom with its own delightful garden, offering hot and cold drinks, sandwiches and cakes.

THE GARDENS

Sandringham House is surrounded by 60 acres of glorious gardens. The formal planting of the Edwardian age has given way to great sweeping glades, bordered by banks and shrubs with splendid specimen trees, to create an informal garden as delightful in autumn as in spring or summer.

SANDRINGHAM CHURCH

This beautiful medieval church, where the Royal Family worship while they are at Sandringham, is open during the visitor season. The highly decorated interior contains a magnificent silver altar and pulpit, together with a very fine 16th-century processional cross and a number of memorials to the Royal Family.

Writing paper

In this paper you will be assessed on your writing skills, including the presentation of your work. Take special care with your handwriting, spelling and punctuation.

Think about the purpose, audience and, where appropriate, the format for your writing.

1 **Your family has won a safari holiday to watch animals in the wild. You are allowed to take one of your friends with you.**

 Write a letter to a friend to explain about the holiday and try to persuade them to come with you.

 In your answer you may like to think about the following:

 - *where you are going*

 - *what you expect to be doing and seeing*

 - *why you have asked this particular friend*

 - *reasons why they should accompany you.*

 - *any other matters you feel are important.*

 The quality of your writing is more important than its length. You should aim to write about one and a half to two sides.

2 **The following is an extract from a letter which appeared in a local paper.**

 'I think the whole world has gone mad. Footballers are bought and sold for huge sums of money; pop stars get more in a week than most people do in a year; some film stars get millions for a bit of acting. Other people are homeless or struggling to pay the rent. At the same time we pay nurses and other professionals stupidly poor wages. The money we pay these so-called 'stars' is obscene and totally unjustified.'

 Write a letter to the newspaper giving your views on this issue.

 In your letter you may like to think about the following:

 - *whether or not the 'stars' are worth the money they get paid*

 - *whether or not it is fair for people like nurses to get a lot less money*

 - *whether or not you agree with the writer of the letter*

 - *any other aspects that you feel are important.*

 You may agree or disagree with this point of view.

 Remember this is a **formal letter** and should be set out appropriately.

 The quality of your writing is more important than its length. You should aim to write about one and a half to two sides.